The term is an apology and an ex~~~
—and often a smokescreen— ~
crimination used to dep
equal rights as America
Semitism did not die witl
the decline of organized ~
country. Instead, it lies im~   ~ın the
American subconscious, rising to the surface in times of tension and, above all,
manifesting itself in hundreds of ways in
daily life.

One aspect of anti-Semitism—discrimination against Jews in the United States
—has assumed patterns and practices that
exist nowhere else in the world, making
it almost a uniquely American phenomenon. It is not readily understandable,
often enough not even identifiable. Yet,
as the authors of this remarkably authori-
tative book show, it is pervasive and real,
affecting much more than the lives of five
and a half million Americans. The authors' concern, of course, is not limited
to Jews. It is all those who suffer under
its patterns, including people who unwittingly or not practice discrimination,

(continued on back flap)

and offering insights on how it might be
excised from the American scene.

Benjaı
Defamat:
written
country
eral cour
of My Bı
explorin
drawn fr
Defamat
ganizatiı
tinuing
educatiı
the nat:
support
cratic /

Anti-
d and
1 this
s gen-
'Some
: book
:rial is
: Anti-
ns or-
a con-
l-scale
B'rith,
rks in
demo-

"SOME OF MY BEST FRIENDS . . ."

"Some of My Best Friends . . ."

by **BENJAMIN R. EPSTEIN**

and **ARNOLD FORSTER**

FARRAR, STRAUS AND CUDAHY / NEW YORK

To

the men and women of the Anti-Defamation League
of B'nai B'rith whose united effort made this book
possible

Authors' Acknowledgment

Extensive surveys of the kind set forth in the following pages require the help of many people—educators, legal scholars, researchers, analysts. To suggest otherwise would be both false and foolish. However, our reason for emphasizing the tremendous contribution of others to this work is less a sense of modesty than an earnest desire to give credit where it is profoundly due. And so—our sincerest appreciation to Oscar Cohen, the Anti-Defamation League's Program Director, for conceiving this book and its area of coverage, and to his aide Oscar Tarcov, who planned the work in its initial stages; to Jacob Sloan, for developing for us his own invaluable research and the data gathered by ADL's Discriminations Department under the direction of Harold Braverman; to Louis Krapin, for endless hours of verifying statistics; to Morton Puner, for his many ADL *Bulletin* articles reporting our agency's findings in the field of religious discrimination (from which we borrowed freely); to Alexander F. Miller, ADL's Community Service Director, and his Regional Staff across the United States, whose daily memoranda and periodic surveys formed many of the foundation stones of this work. Finally, our thanks to Nathan C. Belth, whose reflections on this subject matter have influenced the views expressed in *Some of My Best Friends* . . .

B.R.E. A.F.

Foreword

●

The small scandals of life shock us; the large ones somehow escape our full comprehension and we easily learn to live with them. To cope with such human frailty—in which we all share—the authors of the present volume hit upon a capital idea: They startle us into comprehension of one of the major immoralities of our society by illuminating it with small—but true—tales of what happened to our next door neighbor, or the young man down the street, or someone just like us in the next town.

They have thus added a touch of first rate journalism to sound statistics, sociological analysis and natural moral fervor in a book about that major immorality of our time—anti-Semitism.

The burden of their message is that anti-Semitism in America today expresses itself not in the crudities of a lunatic fringe as in the 1930s, or the comic aping by a self-styled American Nazi of the deadly political game once played by the Hitlerian Nazis.

American anti-Semitism today is expressed in patterns of discrimination built into many of the basic institutions of our society. They are designed to limit, to exclude, to bar Jews from that full participation in the rights, privileges, opportunities and obligations of American life to which all Americans are entitled. That is the big scandal which this book reveals in its myriad details.

Like all scandalous doings, anti-Semitism is most apt to be expressed in furtive ways. Those who practice anti-Semitic discrimination are usually guilt ridden and defensive, because they know that their acts are morally indefensible and seriously damaging to American society's democratic fabric. It is this feeling of guilt that is expressed so often in that unreassuring phrase of assurance which is now doing rueful duty as the title of this book, "Some of my best friends . . ."

HENRY EDWARD SCHULTZ
National Chairman
Anti-Defamation League of B'nai B'rith

Contents

●

"SOME OF MY BEST FRIENDS . . ."

Introduction: An American Problem

●

Scarsdale, New York (population 18,000, average annual family income $17,000), is a quiet town. Lovely shade trees line its winding streets. Spacious homes surrounded by well-tended lawns sit among weeping willow, wisteria, and dogwood. Some of the most influential persons in the United States live here. Scarsdale's schools are among the best in the country. Its country clubs are elegant. Its churches are rich. Its health facilities are excellent. As the local paper, the Scarsdale *Inquirer,* editorialized, "Scarsdale is a community preserved from almost all of life's afflictions."

Among its few afflictions—one by no means unique to Scarsdale—is anti-Semitic discrimination.

No one knows the actual extent or depth of this social disease among the citizens of America's most affluent community, whose population is composed of almost an equal number of Christians and Jews. Most of the time the discriminators are concealed by the secrecy of their acts or by the reluctance of the community—and of the victims themselves

—to lift the veil and expose the ugly face of discrimination that lurks beneath.

In January 1961, however, on the first Sunday after Epiphany, this veil *was* lifted by a courageous clergyman, the Reverend George French Kempsell, Jr., rector of the Church of St. James the Less, a Protestant Episcopal Church in Scarsdale. In his sermon, Father Kempsell shocked his parishioners by saying:

This morning I stand before you with a heart overflowing with sorrow and heartache. Something has happened in this community which I feel must be brought to your attention. . . .

My assistants and I, and many in this congregation here present, have the privilege and pleasure of being members of the Scarsdale Golf Club. As I believe you all know, on the Tuesday after Christmas the annual Holly Ball was held at the Scarsdale Golf Club. What has made me sad is that one young man of this parish, of Jewish parentage, whom I baptized at this font . . . was not considered *acceptable* to be an escort of a young lady of this parish at the Ball. Now, this young lady showed fortitude because, when her friend was not accepted, she withdrew from the Holly Ball—she was not a debutante of this season—she did not "come out" at the Scarsdale Golf Club.

Now I realize that I am dealing with a very complex religious and social issue. I, personally, feel that a member of the Club should be able to take there as his guest anyone who acts with decency, dignity and decorum. . . .

I must, as a priest of this congregation and the pastor of this young man, speak out when a member of my parish, now a Christian, is excluded from the Club. I know that Scarsdale Golf Club is free to work out its own rules and regulations, but I also know that, as a priest of this parish, I must insist that the members of my congregation take a firm stand against a policy which is morally reprehensible. I am not attacking the Club; this is an internal problem of the Club. I am attacking members of my parish, who claim to be Christian, who are *not* acting as Christians should act in their club.

The congregation was surprised by Father Kempsell's exposé. Those who had not known of the discrimination were shocked by the news; those who did were shocked because it had been brought out into the open. But neither group was prepared for what followed. Father Kempsell continued:

I feel it is my responsibility as your pastor to say that anyone who has in any way, by word or in thought or deed, acquiesced with this position of the Scarsdale Golf Club is no longer welcome to receive Holy Communion at this altar—at God's altar—in this parish *until* such time as he has worked out his own peace with God in his own way, whether by using the General Confession in Morning or Evening Prayer, or by making his confession to me or any other priest of the Episcopal Church. I say this to those members of this congregation who may have shared directly in this decision, and I say it to anyone here who in his heart and mind agrees with that decision. . . .

I charge you the members of my congregation to work and pray with me in this matter, and to see that it shall never happen again in our community.

Reactions came quickly. Newspapers in the New York metropolitan area and throughout the country picked up the story. *The New York Times* devoted the better part of four columns to it, with the headline: RECTOR IS PRAISED FOR STAND ON BIAS.

The Scarsdale *Inquirer*'s editorial, entitled "An Unfortunate Silence," lamented that the affair "has focused the attention of the nation on the village to an extent probably unequalled in its history. In the midst of this storm, however, there has been an area of significant quiet. The flood of statements, releases, and expressions of support has included no utterance at all from the Holly Ball Committee or from the Scarsdale Golf Club's Board of Governors."

Father Kempsell's parish remained faithful—and apparently agreed almost unanimously with its rector. Of its eighteen hundred members, only one was reported to have withdrawn from the church.

The parents of the eighteen-year-old girl who refused to go to the Ball and consequently did not make her debut in society that winter, commented: "We have always been proud of our daughter's stand in this matter."

The nineteen-year-old boy who was discriminated against revealed that his father was Jewish and his mother Roman Catholic. He and his brothers had been allowed to select their own religions. The half-Jewish boy, now Episcopalian by choice, remarked:

"Some of my best friends are members of the Scarsdale Golf Club. I bear no grudges against those club people. I would be discriminating myself if I had any hard feelings. I've learned to live with this kind of thing. Anybody with a Jewish parent does."

For ten days the storm raged. On the eleventh day, the Scarsdale Golf Club broke what the town's paper had called its "unfortunate silence," and mailed out a letter of "clarification for future guidance," signed by the Club's president and board of governors.

"Any member of this club may use the facilities of the club to entertain guests and friends of his own choosing," the letter informed 750 member-families.

The storm subsided. There was peace once more in lovely, rich, almost-affliction-free Scarsdale.

When calm finally came, the more sophisticated of the village winked knowledgeably, as if to say: "The veil was lifted for a moment by the strong breeze of public outcry, but when the breeze stops, the veil will fall once again over the discriminators. The vicious face itself—and what makes it—is still with us, even though the veil may now be slightly torn."

The Scarsdale incident had touched some sensitive nerve ends. The young man was Jewish only to the extent that his father had been born a Jew; by religion he was Christian and by preference a member of an Episcopal church. If the Jewish origins of his father made him socially unacceptable—shades of the Nuremberg laws!

That was perhaps the rawest nerve touched. Father Kempsell and others with a knowledge of nineteenth-century European history may well have seen in the incident a reflection of Europe's stratified societies, which slammed the door against Jews who took the road of conversion to Christianity to reach social acceptability and political equality—a road barricaded by the entrenched aristocracy and the military, which raised ethnic issues. One could abjure the beliefs of one's fathers; the fathers themselves could not be denied. The ethnic barriers held and the immediate values of religious conversion were strictly limited.

The tingle of that nerve end, then, was unremarked but not forgotten. What *was* forgotten is the fact that the social discrimination of which the Scarsdale club—and thousands of other clubs like it—are guilty derives largely from an American strain of anti-Semitism. Its roots lie in the 1870–1900 period, when Jews confronted both "the beginnings of social anti-Semitism—a pattern of discrimination—and a crystallization of political anti-Semitism—a politically tinged hostility reflecting power hungers."[1]*

The post-Civil War decades were an era of national social unrest and economic conflict. Perhaps for the first time in American history, the seeds of anti-Semitism had fertile soil in which to grow. At the same time, Jews as a group came to the fore in American life. On one hand, there was the obvious economic success of the German-Jewish immigrants who had begun to arrive in this country with the Forty-Eighters; on the other, an increasing number of Jewish immigrants began to pour into the eastern U.S. cities from Russia and eastern

* Notes will be found on pages 260–263.

Europe after 1880. They were convenient scapegoats: for the agrarian radicals of the Populist movement; for such patrician intellectuals of the East as Henry and Brooks Adams; for the urban poor, largely immigrant stock who had brought their Old-World anti-Semitic prejudices with them.

Unlike as these groups were in ideology, background, and political goals, they had two things in common. They shared a nationalistic jingoism at which they arrived from different directions and for different reasons and they were in conflict with the growing middle class.

The chauvinism of the urban poor was grounded mainly in their rejection of their recent European past. The super-patriotism of the patricians was based on the belief that America had to strike off its European economic chains. And the Populists, corrupting their originally democratic ideology with a nativist outlook, saw all of the nation's troubles coming from abroad.

Perhaps even more important, the industrial age found each of these groups at a disadvantage in the burgeoning middle-class society. The urban poor were cruelly exploited in shop and factory. The aristocrats were increasingly being displaced by the *nouveaux riches* of commerce from their positions of leadership. The agrarian reformers faced a mighty economic struggle with the new industrial plutocracy.

More unlikely allies would be difficult for a single society to produce. They never did learn to understand each other. They remained poles apart, alienated, unhappy with each other, joined only in their common choice of an ethnic-group scapegoat. This explains why anti-Semitism in America, though it ebbed and flowed somewhat in unison with anti-Semitic trends in Europe, never reached the virulence and the tragedy of the European experience. Throughout the first half of the twentieth century, each of these segments of ideology followed its own course. The nativist tradition was reflected in the anti-Semitism of Henry Ford and others, the fulminations against "international bankers" by Father Coughlin, the activities of the Ku Klux Klan and of many lunatic-fringe groups. The impact of organized European anti-Semitism was felt through the German-American Bund, the Christian Front, and other immigrant groups which responded to Nazi propaganda and Old-World hates, but has never been completely centralized in this country.

The established American patricians to some extent built the tradition and began the patterns of discrimination which are the principal concern of these pages—quota systems for colleges and professional schools, racial and religious bars in industry, "gentlemen's agreements" in housing covenants, and exclusionary practices in social institutions which eventually affected the young man in Scarsdale.

The average American's complacency, his lack of knowledge about anti-Jewish discrimination, and his hesitancy to speak out and resist that which he knows to be wrong have compounded the economic and social dislocation to which American Jews are subject today—and have caused additional psychological harm to himself and the nation. Since they are living in a democratic society, Americans of the Jewish faith have set their sights on complete equality with all other citizens. They feel keenly the slights they are forced to accept. Exclusion from full participation in every facet of the life of American society becomes a betrayal of their rights as Americans, as human beings.

For a single moment, Father Kempsell shattered the complacency of his own community—as others have elsewhere from time to time—by forcing his fellow citizens in Scarsdale to look upon the livid face of discrimination in their midst. His act had a cleansing effect. The following pages will lift the veil further on patterns of anti-Jewish discrimination in many places throughout the country—in social relationships, in education, in housing, and in industry. We hope this too will have a cleansing effect.

I. SOCIAL DISCRIMINATION

CHAPTER 1. **The Social Supremacists**

●

"Tennis, anyone—except Negroes and Jews?" asked the tanned young man in the locker room of the fashionable West Side Tennis Club in Forest Hills, New York.

It is doubtful that so unsportsmanlike an invitation was actually ever made in these words, but it might very well have been. The practice of the Club, scene of international championship tennis matches, for years had been one of racial and religious discrimination. As early as 1950 the Club was cited as a discriminatory club.[2]

Little or nothing had been done about it. True, Negro tennis stars (such as Althea Gibson) and Jewish ones (among them Richard Savitt and Sidney Schwartz) had participated in United States championship and Davis Cup challenge rounds played at the Club. But these were paid-admission events. The Club's exclusiveness of membership remained inviolate.

Christian served only to Christian and white volleyed only with white. In the Club's unwritten rule book, the words *social equality* were missing and *love* was a word used only to keep score.

In July 1959, the net curtain that had successfully veiled the select Club's membership practices for so many years was abruptly and dramatically rent by a story that appeared in the international press. Dr. Ralph J. Bunche, United Nations Under Secretary for Special Political Affairs and recipient of the Nobel Peace Prize, and his young son were denied membership in the Club because they were Negro.

As revealed to the press by Dr. Bunche, the dismal story had begun when he had tried to enroll his son in the Club so that the boy could pursue his growing interest in tennis.

"I inquired of friends, some of them members, about the possibility of his joining," Dr. Bunche said. "They told me it didn't look too promising—that there was a policy against Negroes and Jews. So I decided to go to the source and call the Club president."

By telephone, Club president Wilfred Burgland told him that membership was by invitation only, not by application. Bunche replied that a few of his son's schoolmates were members and would extend the invitation. Burgland answered that the Club was private, like a person's home—"where you invite whom you want to." Burgland then revealed that "to his knowledge" there were no Negroes or Jews in the Club nor were there likely to be, and that if the Club accepted a Negro member there would be several hundred resignations.

Dr. Bunche expressed his disbelief and said, "If I were younger I would put in an application myself just for the hell of it."

In reply, Mr. Burgland reminded Dr. Bunche of Club policy.

"Since you assure me I wouldn't be welcome, I am not likely to make an application," Dr. Bunche said.

"You put it very bluntly," Burgland replied.

"But very accurately."

The telephone conversation ended.

In his formal press statement, Dr. Bunche said:

I deliberately revealed this experience only because I find it to be rather shocking in New York City and think citizens of the city and of the country generally are entitled to know about it.

But I keep the story in proper perspective. Neither I nor my son regard it as a hardship or a humiliation. Rather it is a discredit to the Club itself.

It is not, of course, in the category of the disfranchisement, deprival of other rights, segregation and acts of intimidation suffered by many Negroes in the South and of discrimination in employment and housing suffered by most Negroes in the North as well as the South.

But it flows from the same well of racial and religious bigotry. . . .

Immediately following Dr. Bunche's disclosure, city, state, and federal officials, and numerous private groups and individual citizens directed a volley of protest against the Club and its membership policy.

The New York City Commission on Intergroup Relations requested Club officials to appear at a hearing. The Commission had power under the city law that created it in 1955 to "initiate its own investigations of discrimination against any person, group of persons, organizations or corporations, whether practiced by private persons, associations, or corporations."

The chairman declared it was "unthinkable that major international athletic events for which the general public pays admission should be conducted in this city on the grounds of an institution which discriminates in its membership policy."

Moreover, he said, every effort would be made "to see that the city removes any sanctions or facilities provided for public events at this Club as long as it maintains a discriminatory policy."

Abe Stark, then Acting Mayor and President of the New York City Council, appealed to the U.S. Lawn Tennis Association to stop sponsoring matches "played at any club which adheres to such a membership policy." (The Association does not control the policies of its some 1700 member clubs, but insists they keep sponsored tournaments open to all qualified players regardless of race or religion.)

Five U.S. senators wired the USLTA, urging it to transfer the U.S. tennis championships and Davis Cup matches from the West Side Tennis Club. The telegram was signed by Senators Jacob Javits (Republican of New York), Clifford P. Case (Republican of New Jersey), Paul H. Douglas (Democrat of Illinois), Hubert H. Humphrey (Democrat of Minnesota), and Thomas H. Kuchel (Republican of California).

Newspapers everywhere expressed editorial views on the question of discrimination by private clubs and the right of private clubs to determine their own membership policies. These views were far from unanimous.

Said *The New York Times,* in a hard-driving attempt to define the issues at stake:

The West Side Tennis Club . . . is two things; first, it is a private club which, in this land of the free, is entitled to choose its members according to taste; it might require all members to have red hair or to have an intelligence quotient of 150 or more or, possibly, of 100 or less; second, it is a club with some national and international significance as long as it remains the stage on which international and national tennis matches are played.

In its private capacity the Club may choose, as it has done, to deny membership to the son of Ralph Bunche or, in general, to deny membership to any Negro or any person of the Jewish religion. In its public capacity, as an institution with some diplomatic functions, the Club has no right to make these discriminations. . . .

We cannot do anything about the West Side Tennis Club's membership requirements. We may suggest that if it continues to make such requirements it should no longer be considered representative of American public opinion in tennis or in any other area. . . .

There are a number of extravagances we cannot afford in our present struggle to keep Western civilization alive and thriving. One of these extravagances is that stupid and cowardly thing, racial and religious prejudice.

The New York *Herald Tribune* observed: "In its attitude, the West Side Tennis Club is hopelessly out of date, and shockingly unrepresentative of America. Surely some site can be found for these great international tennis matches of which the country need not be ashamed."

Strongly supporting the rights of private clubs to determine their own membership policies was the Baltimore *Sun,* which commented: "The fact that Forest Hills has acquired a quasi-public standing as the site of big national and international tennis tournaments is really beside the point. If an otherwise qualified tennis player were excluded from a tennis tournament to which Forest Hills had granted the use of its facilities on the ground that he or she could not meet the rules for club membership, that would be another matter. But it has not done so. If it were to do so, the proper answer would be to take the tournament somewhere else."

The *Sun* stressed that "it is a mistake to confuse that civil equality which is ordained by the Constitution, and which in the case of American Negroes has been so widely and wrongly disregarded, with the equally valid right of private individuals and private clubs to choose their social companions as they may decide."

The Baltimore paper further noted that "any private club is by definition exclusive in some way or another. If it were not, it would not be a club. It may exclude all but eggheads, all but heavy drinkers, all but left-handed backgammon players, all but white Caucasians with an income of more than $20,000 a year who can trace their ancestry to William the Conqueror. In Baltimore alone there are hundreds, maybe thousands, of private clubs of one sort or another, each with its pet formula for exclusiveness. . . . However idiotic the requirements for membership may be, they are the clubs' affair; and if race enters into the pattern of exclusiveness, so may it."

These were the two basic positions taken by newspapers throughout the country. In effect, what took place was a great public debate on a vital social issue—and an examination of social conscience:

"A person's social life is his own. His individual judgment is supreme and he cannot be required to invite into his home or group anyone not of his choosing—for any reason whatsoever." (Detroit *Free Press*)

"The West Side Tennis Club is a voluntary social organization. As such its members have the legal right under the American system to choose their associates. . . . But in the exercise of that right a voluntary association must also consider the matter of wisdom and of implication perhaps not spelled out by either the Bill of Rights or statute." (*Christian Science Monitor*)

"We're all looking for clubs to join with restricted memberships. It is the easy way to feel superior—which for most of us seems to be the only alternative to feeling inferior." (Detroit *News*)

"There is nothing in law, of course, that can force a private group to accept anyone in membership. But a club is open to public criticism, and properly so, when it bars a whole class of people for racial or similar grounds, regardless of their individual qualifications." (Milwaukee *Journal*)

"The West Side Tennis Club has been assailed in the most violent manner for having its own rules as to membership—

although hundreds of other clubs, North and South, white and colored, also have their own rules. For pious piffle, hypocritical bunk and sanctimonious bilge this Bunche–West Side Club controversy has hit a new low." (Richmond *Times-Dispatch*)

"The West Side Tennis Club has a special obligation to observe the rules of fair play and equality because it is the stage for international and national tennis competition. On its courts many famed Negro and Jewish athletes have appeared in the past." (New York *Journal-American*)

"Any responsible concern for civil liberties should, we think, grant to a private club an inalienable right to the privacy for which it was organized and a corresponding freedom to choose the companions of that privacy whether the choice be good or not. It is not for any man to say whom his neighbor should invite to dinner." (*Sports Illustrated*)

"Racial discrimination, economic and political, is morally wrong. It is equally wrong in the realms of sport." (Boston *Globe*)

"We should, it seems to me, defend all our rights to exclude, slight and eschew anybody in these little clubs." (Margaret Long, Atlanta *Journal*)

"The idea of group social exclusion is insulting and unwholesome. It impoverishes the associations of white Gentiles who practice it unwittingly; it coarsens the characters of the white Gentiles who practice it deliberately." (Des Moines *Register*)

At the height of the national debate, less than a week after the Bunche incident was reported in the press, the governing board of the West Side Club said: "It is the policy of the Club to consider and accept members without regard to race, creed or color." It further said that the Club "presently has members of Oriental and other ancestry and there is representation of the Jewish faith among the membership," but that as far as it knew "no Negro has ever applied for membership."

The Board noted that the West Side Tennis Club "has achieved and holds a status of public importance throughout the sports world, and feels a deep obligation in this respect." It announced that Mr. Burgland—to avoid any more embarrassment—had tendered his resignation as president and that it had been accepted.

Advised of the Board's statement, Dr. Bunche praised its action.

"So far as I am personally concerned, the statement, which is admirably to the point on all counts, winds up the West Side Tennis story. . . .

"This has not been a pleasant experience, and I am glad that it is over. But I will never give aid and comfort to racial and religious intolerance whenever and wherever I encounter it by withholding from the public information that it is entitled to have. In this community, happily, bigotry cannot long stand the heat of public exposure."

Two years later, on July 4, 1961, Robert Lambert, president of the Club, responding to the Anti-Defamation League's inquiry whether the Club's policy was still the same as the Board had stated as a result of the Bunche controversy, wrote:

"The present membership policy of The West Side Tennis Club, I wish to assure you, is to consider and accept members without regard to race, creed or color."

Tennis, everyone?

Discriminatory practices by social clubs, long recognized as a pervasive pattern among proverbially gregarious Americans, was dramatically and publicly challenged in the summer of 1961 by the U.S. Attorney General and several other important public figures who resigned from the Metropolitan Club, probably the most distinguished club in Washington, D.C. Mr. Robert Kennedy's act was of a piece with the action of

Dr. Ralph Bunche in challenging the action of the West Side Tennis Club for refusing membership to his son. As will be shown later, back in 1956, the Anti-Defamation League publicly challenged the tax exemption of the Merchants Club in New York City, which as a social club barred Jews but for tax advantages called itself a business club. A year earlier Mrs. Eleanor Roosevelt, invited to speak at a community Brotherhood Week function in Lancaster, Pa., canceled her appearance at the last moment. She found that the local club at which the meeting was to be held, barred Jews from membership and even as guests except on this occasion.

Why these public challenges? Clubs which discriminate on religious and racial grounds have traditionally taken, and won acceptance for, the position that the social club is an extension of one's own parlor. Thus, if a man has a right to choose whom he will invite into his home, he also has the right to choose whom he will admit to his club.

Those who issue the challenge say that they are concerned only when the right of privacy is invoked to the detriment of the common good and when it runs counter to public policy. They are primarily concerned with discriminatory clubs that become important factors in a community's or industry's power structure. They are secondarily concerned with clubs which, because of their special character, take on quasi-public functions. Finally, they are concerned with those which, because of their positions of prestige, tend to foster undemocratic social patterns in the total community.

The Anti-Defamation League generally associates itself with the views of the challengers. It arrived at that position from its own observations of the phenomenon of the discriminatory social club and from the sociological researches into various aspects of the problem that are only now beginning to inform public opinion. These researches reveal new dimensions in the discriminatory practices by private clubs.

If the seat of power in any community discriminates against

Jews, it may sound a note that will be taken up by others in the community. The industrialist who is a member of the "power structure" club will be confirmed in his negative view about Jewish plant managers; the plant managers in turn will find it more expedient not to employ Jewish subordinates. Lower echelon civic groups, ears closely attuned to the note from on high, will find sanction for similar exclusions. The university, upon whose board of trustees sit members of the discriminatory club, will not protest a quota system, the fraternities will mimic their elders in exclusionary practices. Thus may a new generation, while still in its formative years, be schooled in the ways and benefits of social discriminations.

Clearly, the problems created by such exclusionary practices are not merely social; they are more frequently economic, political and sociological. The ultimate victim is not the man reaching toward the seat of power or toward the prestige of upper level social acceptance. Rather it is the youth who finds he is barred from job or school (and when he is older, from a home) simply and solely because he is Jewish.

Comparatively few of the substantial number of exclusionary clubs are strategic elements in the power structure of a community; most simply foster undesirable and undemocratic social practices. These may only be minor sources of irritation, singly, but they represent in their totality a formidable expression of anti-Semitic attitudes. They are the result of social and economic forces which have been operating on the American scene for many decades—and they represent the feelings of millions of individual Americans.

Obviously, there must be concern with the irrational exclusion of Jews from clubs which by reasonable test are secular in purpose and program. For such exclusion represents a philosophy of racism. It not only gratuitously wounds the "outs," but it nurtures and re-inforces in the minds of the "ins" the notion that Jews should be shunned. In short, if the democratic goal is sane intergroup relations and healthy attitudes, discrimination by such clubs, however small they may be, must be treated. One can no more disregard the development of anti-Semitic prejudices in the club room than in any other facet of our society.

It is common knowledge, of course, that the practices of clubs which bar Jews have had their concomitant in the establishment by Jews of separate club facilities; this, too, must be a matter for concern.

It should be apparent, however, that those groups which are organized for clearly religious purposes have an unchallengeable right to impose religious requirements for membership. There can be no question of the right of a Newman Club to limit membership to Catholics, the men's club of a temple to a Jew, the Westminster Fellowship to Presbyterians. Thus, too, B'nai B'rith, the Knights of Columbus, the Epworth League, all frankly religious in purpose and orientation, are beyond reproach for their sectarian membership requirements.

While there have been depth studies of discrimination in private clubs in recent years, there had been no effort to determine how widespread the practice was. In 1961, therefore, the Anti-Defamation League proceeded to fill that gap by making a frankly statistical study. Its report was completed just as this book was going to press and the findings are significant.

To determine the extent of the religious discrimination, the League surveyed a representative list of clubs which could reasonably be termed a national cross-section. The criterion for selection was whether the clubs employed professional managers. A list of clubs maintained by a group of managers in the private club field was used for the sample. The total number of such clubs was 1,332 but for purposes of the study 44 Armed Forces clubs on the list were excluded, leaving a balance of 1,288 clubs with essentially civilian memberships.

The 1,288 clubs were situated in 46 states and District of Columbia. Only four states—Alaska, Maine, New Hampshire and Vermont—were not represented in the survey group because there were none on the professional list. The numbers of clubs in the other states ranged from one each in North Dakota and Wyoming to 159 in New York State.

The private clubs on which information was sought were broadly of two types; first, "city clubs" which were defined as clubs physically situated within cities or towns. The second, "country clubs," were defined as those located in suburban and rural areas which had the facilities normally associated with country clubs—golf course, tennis courts, swimming pools, and other sport facilities.

The survey was conducted by the staff of the Anti-Defamation League and the first step was to establish the status of each club under examination. Three categories were set up: high prestige or power structure clubs; those which enjoyed average acceptance; and those which were considered of little or no importance. This information was obtained by interviewing knowledgeable people and polling a cross-section of community opinion.

Thereafter, a determination was made for each club as to whether it discriminated on the basis of religion. An identification of "non-discrimination" was made if the club accepted as members Christians and Jews without regard to religion. If they either barred Jews or had a quota for Jewish membership, the club was considered discriminatory; it was then designated a "Christian club." The field researchers were asked to distinguish between clubs that barred Jews absolutely and those that admitted Jews on a limited basis. In the same way, identification was made of "Jewish clubs" which either barred Christians or had quotas for Christian members.

Finally, wherever a club was identified as a "Christian club" or a "Jewish club," the field researcher sought to establish whether the restrictions were official (in the club's constitution or by-laws) or unofficial (informal, gentlemen's agreement).

Of the 1,288 clubs on which information was sought data was received on 1,152 or almost 90 per cent. The remaining 10 per cent represented clubs that had gone out of existence or about which, for a variety of reasons, information was not available.

The 1,152 clubs on which facts were obtained had a total estimated membership of 700,000 and were located in 46 states and the District of Columbia. Almost 33 per cent (371 clubs) of them were non-discriminatory, erecting no religious barriers to membership. *On the other hand, 67 per cent (781 clubs) practiced religious discrimination of which 691 were "Christian clubs" which either barred Jews completely or imposed a limitation upon the number of Jews that could join—60 per cent of all clubs examined. Of the 781 discriminatory clubs, 90 were "Jewish clubs" which either barred Christian membership or imposed limitations upon Christians—almost 8 per cent of all clubs studied.*

Of the 691 "Christian clubs" about 80 per cent (555 clubs) barred Jews completely, while the remainder, about 20 per cent (136 clubs), limited Jewish membership to small numbers. Of the 90 "Jewish clubs," about 95 per cent of the group (85 clubs), barred Christian members completely; the other 5 per cent admitted Christians in small numbers.

Of the 781 discriminatory clubs, about 90 per cent (696 clubs) maintained their restrictions "unofficially"—without religious proscriptions in their constitutions or by-laws. The restrictive practices of these clubs were carried out informally through gentlemen's agreements, etc. The remaining restrictive clubs, about 10 per cent, were said to maintain their restrictions "officially"—by constitution or by-laws

Of the 1,152 institutions surveyed, 349 were city clubs with an estimated membership of 300,000. With respect to "status," more than 60 per cent enjoyed the highest in their communities; 30 per cent had average acceptance; about 10 per cent were considered to have little standing. Over 40 per cent of the city clubs (147) were non-discriminatory, erecting no religious barriers to membership. On the other hand, almost 60 per cent of these clubs (202) practiced religious discrimination.

Of the 1,152 institutions surveyed, 803 were country clubs with an estimated 400,000 members. On the subject of status again, more than 60 per cent were regarded as "tops" in their areas; 33 per cent had average acceptance; 7 per cent were considered to have little standing. Here, there was a smaller percentage of clubs that were non-discriminatory; only 28 per cent (224) erected no religious barriers to membership. But 72 per cent (579) of the country clubs did practice religious discrimination as against only 60 per cent of the city clubs.

The ADL analyzed in several other ways the data it accumulated for its study. It ascertained, for example, the arithmetic of private club discrimination according to geographic area, by the size of the towns involved, by the character (athletic or otherwise) of the city clubs researched.

Finally, the ADL concluded that the religious discriminatory practices engaged in by 67 per cent of the clubs it studied indicate a serious failure on the part of the community at large to accept fellow Americans socially on the basis of individual merit and worth. If private clubs are the measuring rod, there is a far higher quotient of social discrimination in America than there is discrimination in the areas of education, employment and housing.

An appreciation of the workings of social discrimination is basic to an understanding of anti-Semitism in the United States today. In current professional usage among those concerned with American intergroup relations, the term *social discrimination* refers generally to the attitudes and practices leading to the exclusion of minorities from resort hotels, civic and recreational clubs, fraternal organizations, and, in a broad sense, from organized social intercourse on the personal level.

Certainly, this description considerably limits both parts of the term. The *Shorter Oxford English Dictionary* lists eight meanings for the word *social,* of which we are employing only the fourth: "Marked or characterized by mutual intercourse, friendliness, or geniality; enjoyed, taken, spent, etc., in company with others, esp. with those of a similar class or kindred interests."

This limitation is deliberate. No one would gainsay that *all* discrimination is social, insofar as it affects people in their role as members of groups in society, rather than as unique and distinctive individuals. But we are stressing the *anti*social character of one aspect of social behavior in the United States. The *Encyclopedia of the Social Sciences* states the contradiction:

Social discrimination involves the unequal treatment of equals.

The ambiguity surrounding the second part of the term, *discrimination,* is more important—and far more emotion-laden. Since we shall be speaking of discrimination constantly throughout this book, it will be useful to describe at greater length the way we are defining and employing it.

Many people who are content with the existence of social discrimination like to defend the *status quo* by referring to the everyday, legitimate sense of the word *discrimination*— a kind of technique for reacting in different ways to different persons, objects, or situations. They are quite willing to admit that this kind of discrimination, often implying the reactor's superior standards, sometimes indicates a feeling of superiority on his part. But they can see nothing wrong with knowing that one is superior to others and acting on that assumption, though this may seem an unwarranted presumption to those being discriminated against. A favorite analogy cited in this connection is that of the wine connoisseur, who is "discriminating" in his judgment of wines. What is wrong, the argument runs, with being similarly discriminating in one's personal associations?

Those who argue along this line fail or refuse to recognize that when "discrimination" is applied to individuals as individuals it is perfectly acceptable; applied to individuals as symbolic of social *groups,* it involves something much more than a difference in taste. Then we have

. . . discrimination . . . prejudicial treatment; any difference in action premised upon prejudice, or upon the class or category by which an individual is typed, rather than upon his relative characteristics: e.g., RACE DISCRIMINATION, treating a person in a given way because of his race or *ethnic group.*[3]

This is not to say that all discrimination is accompanied by prejudice—but it is in the kind of discrimination we are referring to. On the other hand, prejudice need not always result in active discrimination. A social psychologist has put the distinction plainly:

What people actually do in relation to groups they dislike is not always directly related to what they think or feel about them. Two employers, for example, may dislike Jews to an equal degree. One may keep his feelings to himself and may hire Jews on the same basis as any workers—perhaps because he wants to gain good will for his factory or store in the Jewish community. The other may translate his dislike into his employment policy, and refuse to hire Jews. Both men are prejudiced, but only one of them practices *discrimination.*[4]

Presumably, if our wine connoisseur is discriminating *against* anything it is against bad wines, something that as an expert he is entitled to do.

But social discrimination based on group prejudice is

hostile in origin, irrational in practice, and malicious in effect. If the social discriminators we are referring to in this book were merely claiming their right to choose their personal friends on an individual basis, with no offense intended for the many persons not chosen, they would not be open to criticism. But many social discriminators systematize their hostility to various groups by adopting arbitrary standards of distinction that label all members of certain groups desirable and all others undesirable. These standards are demonstrably false, the results of their application injurious, and the resulting social discrimination is indefensible.

Group social discrimination works in subtle ways that frequently appeal—unfortunately—to deep-seated human needs. Consequently, it is not always apparent that it *is* irrational, that anyone is harmed in any but superficial respects, or that the larger consequences for American society as a whole are of the first magnitude.

During the last decade of social and psychological research, however, it has become clear that the contemporary exclusion of American Jews and other groups from various forms of social intercourse affects not only the excluded, but two other groups as well: (1) the active excluders, who vigorously carry out exclusionist policies by seeing to it that Jews are *not* invited to join a club, though they may visit as occasional guests; and (2) the "innocent bystanders," who accept the club's rules (written or tacit) and go along with the crowd— that is, with public opinion as defined or molded by the active excluders.

One argument used to justify the practice of social discrimination is flat denial that there is any analogy between the deleterious results of group discrimination when it involves the denial of employment, housing, or education, and the implications of "keeping minorities out of places they really don't want to go to"—it is for their own benefit: "They'll be happier among their own." When the counter-argument that it is up to Americans to decide where they will be happier is raised, the advocates of the *status quo* are quick to point to the "facts": Is there, or is there not, a "natural and inevitable" tendency for American Jews to move within their own private circles (their alleged "clannishness"); to prefer their own golf clubs, fraternal orders, professional and veterans' organizations?

This of course raises the question of the chicken and the egg in the field of American anti-Semitism, of historical and psychological genesis: Which comes first—externally enforced segregation of Jews in enclaves of their own or self-segregation to perpetuate a unique way of life? Historians and psychologists differ; here we are concerned primarily with pointing up the practice and noting effects of social discrimination rather than with the *why* of it.

The American Jew, confronted with the actuality of social exclusiveness, deliberately withdraws himself from many forms of personal association with non-Jews in anticipation of rejection. To avoid the probability or at least the possibility of being blackballed by his non-Jewish neighbors, since it would be painful to his self-esteem, he enters a private association of his own. Often his reaction is extreme. The American Jewish victim of social discrimination (actual or potential) goes into competition with his excluder. He works hard to make his own private association superior to the one he cannot join. He overvalues himself in relation to the others who, in refusing him the pleasure of their company, are seeking to devalue him.

Louis Wirth, in his classic 1928 study of the "ghetto" in Chicago, depicts the stages of personal relationship between Jew and non-Jew in the United States: first, the ghetto situation; second, the transitional experimental stage, when the ex-ghetto Jew tries to associate freely with his non-Jewish fellow Americans; third, the rejection (real or anticipated);

and, finally, the retreat to a self-imposed new ghetto. result is that

Prejudice from without has revived the ghetto wall, less visib perhaps, than before, but not less real. . . . As the Jew emerges from the ghetto and takes on the character of humanity in the outside world, the ghetto declines. But as this freedom is restricted . . . distances between Jews and non-Jews arise; and the retreat to the ghetto sets in. . . . The Jews became exclusive because at a certain period in their history they were excluded.[5]

The fact that the damage done to American Jews through social discrimination is more psychological than economic does not minimize it; the contrary is the case. Students of modern American society have gone to some pains to scotch the notion that Americans, because of their concern with material things, are "unspiritual." Rather, they have pointed out, we are all highly idealistic, sensitive to criticism, and terribly anxious to present a favorable image of ourselves— both at home and to the world. Prestige and status are today as important to Americans as a full pocketbook, sometimes more important. One of the reasons there is so much concern with mental health in this country is because such *feelings* are so important to us.

It is important that those who justify their refusal to permit Jews to share their "privacy" understand what this refusal is costing the total society in psychological and mental-health terms. The discriminatory exercise of the "right to voluntary personal association" is not a carefree matter; it is accompanied by certain powerful emotions that can wreak havoc with the exerciser's psyche:

In ancient times, it was not uncommon to beat, steal from, enslave, or curse a group of people; it was rare for personal association to be thought improper or indecent. . . . The emotions attending social discrimination—and there are always emotions attending it, unlike other forms of discrimination—appear to be *fear* and *disgust,* or both.[6]

And there actually may be nothing voluntary about social discrimination, as William Peters noted in a *Redbook* article:

If [the Johnsons] wish to live in their New York suburb—or any of the hundreds of American residential communities like it— if they wish to belong to the only country club, if Dorothy wants to participate in the only women's club or have her daughter attend its only dancing class, they must join the discriminators, like it or not. For the admission requirements were set long before they came to the community.[7]

Prearranged social discrimination undermines another favorite argument of habitual social discriminators—that Americans are accountable to no one for their voluntary preferences in companions. To the extent that the active discriminators impose their standards on the innocent bystanders, forcing them to desist from association with minority-group members, to that extent they are depriving the innocent bystanders of freedom of volition. The innocent becomes a confederate—a "polite discriminator"—both because he is too polite to object and because he politely ignores (but accepts) exclusionary policies and practices. Why stir up trouble?

Yet the polite discriminator suffers, too: first, because *his* freedom of choice of personal associations is being abridged without his prior consent and second, because basically he knows that what he is concurring in conflicts with the ideals of his religion and his nation. The "American Creed," in Gunnar Myrdal's words, considers all men equally entitled to the opportunity for participation in every avenue of life "regardless of race, nationality or creed." The "American Religion," described by Will Herberg, regards all faiths as equally sacred, equally valid alternative forms of a generalized egalitarian religion—the implication being that "to be a Protestant, Catholic, or a Jew are today the alternative ways

served. "It has a small, intimate bar, flowers on the mantel, a wood fire in the lounge, and no bulletin boards. It is *de rigueur* to keep out anything bordering on commercialization of the Club. Occasionally a member wants to use the Club's name in connection with some new textile. But this idea is always sat upon. The Club is especially proud of its century-long traditions."

Although one of the Club's strongest traditions has been its exclusion of Jews, many of its members reject the idea that they personally are anti-Semitic. They are quick to point out that some of their best friends—and customers—are Jewish. But for nearly a century no member has been known seriously to have challenged the anti-Jewish tradition that began in the 1870s, when the suddenly rich textile merchants, heady with post-bellum prosperity but rejected by the older landed gentry of New York, began reaching out for social standing. This is the historic origin of the caste system of the Merchants Club. For some time it maintained a Protestant homogeneity, eventually progressing to its "Christians-only" policy.

Over the years, many in the cotton-textile industry have questioned the propriety of this policy. Merchants Club members have argued that their club is a private group that has a right to set up its own standards for membership. They say that the Club is a closely knit, almost family-type social organization. They also report that no member has been derelict in his financial obligations to the Club for the past thirty years and that only one member has been disciplined for improper conduct in recent years. "And that was because the fellow was in his cups," a member explained.

These arguments might be somewhat impressive if the Merchants Club itself had not made strenuous efforts to repudiate the social-club designation and involved itself in litigation to prove it a quasi-public, strictly business organization. This has resulted in the special paradox of the Merchants Club. Upon closer examination, the paradox becomes

quite understandable. The Club has a dual personality because as a business organization it has favorable tax advantages and as a social club it can attempt to justify its restric-
tive-membership practices.

The inconsistent situation dates back to 1928, when the
Club asked for repayment of taxes paid on members' dues
totaling more than twenty thousand dollars on the ground
that it was not a social club. (The United States Internal
Revenue Code provides for federal taxation of dues and
initiation fees collected by social, sports, and athletic clubs.)
The Commissioner of Internal Revenue allowed the claim,
which was repaid the Club by the government in June 1934.

Eight years later the Internal Revenue Bureau took another look at the Club, and in November 1942 and January
1943 officially notified it that as of January 1, 1943, it would
be considered a social club and that its receipts would be
taxable.

Less than two weeks later the Merchants Club amended its
purpose clause to read:

"The purpose of the Club shall be to establish and maintain quarters and accessories convenient to its members'
places of business wherein such members, their associates,
clients and business friends may obtain their mid-day meals
amid quiet surroundings and have available private rooms
suitable for business conferences."

Two years later the Merchants Club brought action against
the United States government to recover some twelve thousand dollars in taxes that had been levied in the intervening
two years. Conspicuous by its absence in the brief submitted
by the Merchants Club to the Court of Claims was the fact
that Jews were unwelcome as members or guests.

The Club argued that it "is even less 'social' than an
ordinary businessman's luncheon club" and that it has "no
important social features."

The Club's brief bolstered this argument by citing these findings, established in the preliminary hearings:

"The Club has no facilities for the playing of games, either social or athletic. There are no billiard or pool tables, or other such facilities. No games of any sort are ever played on the Club premises nor have such games ever been played. The Club rules specifically prohibit the playing of such games. . . .

"The Club never holds parties, open houses, dances or any similar functions. . . ."

Finally, to refute the idea that the Club was a group bound together by social ties, the brief insisted that the Club was ". . . an important and necessary cog in the business of distributing the nation's output of cotton-textiles . . . performing a strictly utilitarian function . . . a function which is comparable to that performed on a more elaborate scale by the New York Stock Exchange in the marketing of securities."

To advance the Club's claim of being a major cog in the wheels of the textile industry, the brief further stated that:

The Merchants Club occupies an important place in the cotton-textile industry. It is the quasi-official center and headquarters of the selling end of the cotton-textile industry. It is the only common meeting place for members of that industry and its membership includes the top executives of substantially all the commission merchants dealing in the primary cotton-textile market. . . .

The Club is used regularly for meetings held to deal with industry problems. The industry codes under the N.R.A. and A.A.A. were negotiated at a series of meetings in the Club and most of the standard trade practices of the textile business have been developed at meetings in the Club.

Membership in the Club is regarded as a business necessity by the top executives of the commission houses dealing in the primary cotton-textile market and a commission house not represented in the Club is at a decided disadvantage. . . .

There is no official stock exchange for the marketing of cotton-textiles and the Club serves as a clearing house for all information dealing with the industry.

Many in the industry have pointed out that these claims were exaggerated. If they were not, they ask, how could so many Jewish businessmen in the industry have survived and prospered? Then, hoisting the Club on its own petard, they ask a key—and damning—question: If membership in the Club is so necessary for a successful pursuit of cotton-textile business, how can the Club justify its exclusion of an entire group of businessmen because of their religion? Regardless of the demonstrable bigotry involved, does not the Club's policy deny business opportunities to Jews that are granted to non-Jews?

At any rate, the Club's arguments were persuasive enough to win it a favorable verdict and a refund of $12,016.81, plus interest.

This firmly established the paradox of the Merchants Club. On one hand the government now agreed with the Club's own estimate of itself—that it is strictly a utilitarian business organization. On the other hand, for ninety years the Club's members have defended the policy of exclusion of Jews on the ground that the Club is a social organization whose members enjoy a close family-type relationship, and that men have a right to group themselves on the basis of common religious beliefs.

In an attempt to unravel this contradiction, on May 14, 1956, the Anti-Defamation League wrote the following letter to Malcolm S. Black, president of the Merchants Club:

In all candor, we must tell you that we have been receiving questions from many individuals, both inside and outside the cotton-textile industry, who, for reasons of their own, desire an evaluation by the Anti-Defamation League of whether the Merchants Club bars Jews from membership and the use of its facilities. We are under an obligation to answer these queries, and under an equal obligation not to do the Merchants Club any injustice.

Obviously, if the Merchants Club is a social club whose basis for existence is religious homogeneity, the propriety of its membership policies must be considered within the context of rights of social privacy.

We feel that an intelligent approach to this complex problem requires a personal meeting with you and any other officers of the Merchants Club concerned with this matter. Hopefully, such a discussion, undertaken in a spirit of honest and frank exploration, may prevent misunderstanding.

If this suggestion is acceptable, we will be happy to meet with you and your colleagues at any time and place suitable to you.

There was no answer.

Another letter written by the League on June 5 to the president of the Club again proposing a meeting was also ignored.

To this day, the paradox of the Merchants Club remains: It is a business organization for the purpose of tax exemption in its relationship with the United States Internal Revenue Bureau, and a nonbusiness organization for the purpose of social and religious exclusivity in its relationship with the community.

There we have the puzzling anomaly of the Merchants Club—neither fish nor fowl—but a substantial organization approaching its century mark without having been sullied by the presence on its rolls of a "nonacceptable" member.

Abraham Cahan, for more than half a century the editor of an important Jewish newspaper in the United States, summed up the attitude of many Jewish leaders when he said in 1890:

We have no Jewish question in America. The only question we recognize is the question of how to prevent the emergence of the "Jewish questions" here.[11]

Cahan was an immigrant from Czarist Russia, familiar

with real persecution of Jews—political, economic, and social.
He was no pollyanna, by any means, but a radical socialist
who came to America, he says in his autobiography, to help
found a socialist commonwealth in the New World. But the
facts of his new country's life gradually converted him into a
moderate reformer, a supporter of Roosevelt's New Deal in
the editorial pages of his *Jewish Daily Forward* of New York.
We may therefore regard Cahan's assertion as representative
of serious thought, not wishful thinking. There is no cause
for alarm, Cahan is telling us: there is, however, need to
foresee the possibilities of cause for alarm. The Jewish situation in the United States is secure—but that security is not
self-perpetuating; it requires constant alertness.

In the 1960s, it is the consensus of informed people, on
the basis of general surveys and of specific community studies,
that American Jews have more than held their own in this
country—they have made healthy progress. W. L. Warner
and P. S. Lunt are explicit in comparing the economic accomplishments of a group of Jewish immigrants with the
success of other ethnic groups in the same community. Reporting on the status system of a modern New England community (Newburyport, Massachusetts, called "Yankee City"
in their book), they pointed out in 1942 that the Jews of
Yankee City had moved upward faster economically than the
other groups who immigrated at the same time—even faster
than the Irish, who had arrived in America a full generation
earlier.[12] This rapid success Warner and Lunt attribute
primarily to Jewish experience in urban living in the Old
Country where, during the course of centuries, Jews had
learned commercial and professional skills applicable to the
American urban scene. Immigrants from other ethnic groups
—South Italian in origin, for example—had fewer skills to
apply, coming as they did from a rural environment; their
rise and that of their children up the economic and occupational ladder was slower.

On the other hand, Louis Wirth throws an interesting sidelight on any comparison between the urban background of the immigrant Jew and the rural-background immigrants from South Italy:

When we characterize the Jews as an urban people . . . we do so with the important qualification that the Jews of Eastern Europe occupied until recently the status of village people.[13]

This qualification anticipates the need for a more penetrating explanation, which Nathan Glazer attempts to provide in his book *American Judaism*. After summarizing the data describing the sociological characteristics of the second generation of American Jewish immigrants that aided them in their rise in American society, Glazer develops a somewhat wider concept of the source of these characteristics. He associates them with traditional Jewish emphasis on values that parallel those accepted by middle-class American society as a whole.[14] Max Weber argued in his *Ancient Judaism* that the values associated with success in middle-class pursuits originated in a certain kind of religious outlook—the outlook of Calvinism, which so strongly influenced the early Protestant settlers in the American colonies.[15] Glazer traces a parallel Jewish religious outlook back to an earlier period in Jewish history, the Hellenistic Age in the Near East, when Phariseeism triumphed over Saduceeism.

Certainly, American Jews as a whole have worked hard to achieve a high standard of living, and they have been generally successful in that effort. It is difficult to document this success on a national scale in the same way it is possible to substantiate, for example, the limited recent national growth of Negro economic strength. The reason is both statistical and descriptive: the United States Census Bureau decennial and interim surveys of the population of the United States ask the color of the respondent's skin but not his religious affiliation.

We do have acceptable data comparing local Jewish occupational patterns with those of non-Jews, in the form of self-studies conducted by specific Jewish communities. When the findings of these studies are compared with the statistics of the Census Bureau for the population of the locality as a whole, the results are probably trustworthy; they are certainly illuminating.

Alvin Chenkin has summarized the findings of self-studies of three medium-sized Jewish communities—Canton, Ohio (1955); Des Moines, Iowa, and Washington, D.C. (1956). These studies, the most recent of their kind, reported that four out of every five Jews employed in these cities (where fewer than 50,000 Jews lived) held jobs ranging from semi-skilled to highly skilled.

Eighty per cent or more of the labor force in each of the three communities were in the professional and technical, managerial and proprietarial, clerical and sales occupations. These proportions were far higher than those found in the general population.[16]

The Jewish community of San Francisco and its environs has also recently completed a self-study. The figures relating to the Jewish occupation pattern in this long-established Jewish community, where social discrimination is considered to be minimum, are particularly interesting.[17]

	San Francisco	Peninsula	Marin
Prof. and Semi-Prof.	25.1	33.3	38.7
Proprietor, Manager	26.6	25.0	28.3
Clerical, Sales	35.1	27.7	18.8
Craftsmen, Foremen	5.5	7.4	nil
Operatives	1.8	nil	3.8
Service Workers	3.0	2.8	8.5
Laborers	.7	1.9	nil
Unemployed	2.2	1.9	1.9
	100.0	100.0	100.0

The figures reveal that in San Francisco and the two adjoining communities of Marin County and the Peninsula nearly 87 per cent of the Jewish labor force were in the three upper categories—a higher proportion than in Chenkin's smaller communities. These statistics give strong confirmation of both the Jewish movement into higher economic status and the importance of residence in a relatively free general community. It is interesting to note that ever since the city was founded Jews in the San Francisco area have had wide freedom to integrate socially in the community, with the result that its Jewish residents have had more opportunities for occupational advancement.

(How have American Jews achieved their relative success? The customary road to self-improvement in the United States is through education—an activity highly valued among Jews since the days of the Palestinian and Babylonian academies at the beginning of the first millennium of the Common Era.) Chenkin provides specific data that show how Jews in these communities pursued education in comparison with their non-Jewish neighbors:

One of the most striking characteristics of the Jewish population noted by many observers was the intense drive for education. . . . High proportions of the Jewish population went to college or took post-graduate work.[18]

Chenkin further reported that of the Jewish population over twenty-five years of age, Canton showed 36 per cent as having attended college or done postgraduate study, Des Moines 37 per cent, Washington, D.C., 41 per cent. In Canton, 36 per cent had attended the first year of college, compared with 12 per cent of the general population; in Des Moines 38 per cent, compared with 19 per cent of the general population.

American Jews have had some difficulty in getting medical, legal, engineering, and accounting training in colleges and universities. In the main, however, they have overcome those difficulties. They have managed to complete their training at institutions of higher education, which is indispensable for advancement in a modern technological society such as that of the United States.

Inevitably, (the fairly rapid rise of American Jews up the economic ladder has aroused social aspirations corresponding to their new status) For instance, a physician wants a home in what is considered a fairly fashionable neighborhood and prefers the company of persons he regards as his cultural peers. This is one of the points at which American Jews are confronted with social discrimination. The non-Jewish colleague is quite willing to work alongside the Jewish doctor—sometimes in Jewish-sponsored hospitals open to the general public—but he is often reluctant to invite his Jewish colleague into a social club or to have him live next door.

The Jews' movement upward in the American situation has brought many of them into the position of anticipating problems that other minority ethnic or racial groups have not yet found so pressing. American Negroes are still largely concerned with obtaining entrance to those aspects of the country's economy that Jews have already entered—the professions, the sciences, business, and skilled labor. Hence, on the whole the other groups are not yet interested in pressing for absolute freedom of social intercourse.

For the time being, therefore, the American Jew finds himself in a unique position. He has been most decisively singled out for social exclusion in many places. Paradoxically, he was trapped into these restrictions because of the speed with which he adjusted to the American way of life. He fitted into the economy quickly and well—but in the opinion of those who arrived here ahead of him, he did so before he had sufficiently (for them) rid himself of his European "mannerisms" or moved far enough away from his ghetto beginnings.

CHAPTER 3.   **America's Vacation Playgrounds**

●

Two short weeks before its scheduled 1954 convention at the
Camelback Inn of Phoenix, Arizona, the National Association of Attorneys General canceled its elaborate arrangements
for its meeting in Arizona and met instead in West Virginia.
The reason for its action was the restricted guest-admission
policy of the famous resort hotel. Seven years later, Camelback manager Jack Stewart confirmed in writing that the
policy of the Inn was no longer the same. He now made it
clear that "religion is not and will not be the criterion" with
respect to his guests.

What happened in the intervening seven years? The
Camelback Inn management apparently concluded that prevailing sentiment in America required a change in the hotel's
policy. Without question, the key person in the situation,
Jack Stewart, had arrived at this decision completely on his
own, not being the kind of man to knuckle under to pressure.
How did Stewart come to his decision?

In December 1956, Louis S. Vosburgh, president of the
Lincoln Institute in Cleveland, decided to take a brief winter

holiday with his wife at the Camelback Inn, situated in a delightful vacation area that has justifiably been called the Valley of the Sun.

Like most people preparing for a holiday, the Vosburghs looked forward eagerly to a time devoted to rest and carefree pleasure. As it turned out, they were given a most uncarefree indoctrination into the practices of discriminatory resorts.

When Mr. Vosburgh wrote for reservations to Camelback Inn, he was unaware that for many years the Inn had systematically barred would-be guests who were, or appeared to be, Jewish. Since he was not a member of the Jewish faith, he was unprepared for this new experience.

When the Inn management received Mr. Vosburgh's letter, Jack Stewart, the manager, offered him accommodations, but asked if he "would be kind enough to give us your church and club affiliations."

Mr. Vosburgh replied: "We are churchgoers to some extent and have had two or three affiliations in the past, but at the present time neither Mrs. Vosburgh or myself is a member of any particular church. With reference to club affiliations, we have, generally speaking, not been joiners. I have been a member of the Mid-Day Club, which is an affiliate of the Cleveland Chamber of Commerce, for years. In recent years I have held membership in the Clearwater Yacht Club as well as the Carlouel Club, both of Clearwater, Florida."

The management of the Inn responded promptly, assuring Mr. Vosburgh that he and his wife "are the kind of people we would be very happy to have among our guests."

Still, the name Vosburgh apparently still roused the management's fears. The letter to Mr. Vosburgh continued: "However, since your letter actually did not give us the information desired, we wonder if you would be kind enough to tell us your nationality. Unfortunately, we do not know the clubs you mention, and while this is not our personal feeling in the matter, our guests demand that we cater only to those who can be entirely a part of their tastes and interests."

Rankled by the labored amenities and inquisitorial methods, Mr. Vosburgh wrote back:

"I feel compelled to tell you that in all my life it has never been necessary to subject myself to such close scrutiny in order to obtain hotel accommodations for a short period of ten days. Furthermore, I doubt if the majority of a strictly high-class clientele would subject themselves to such third-degree tactics. Do you find that these methods protect you very completely against undesirables? I'm wondering if they don't drive some of the most desirable away from the hotel.

"I happen to own a motel in Florida. We too strive for a certain class level in our guests—but we never subject newcomers to such close scrutiny as to enquire of their nationality, etc.

"You now ask for my nationality. . . . I certainly shall be interested in knowing those nationalities in this country which you consider constitute the elite.

"As for myself, my ancestry is Holland Dutch, the original Vosburgh family having settled in Albany, New York, in the year 1642. My mother was Pennsylvania Dutch with a little French thrown in. If this is objectionable—I'm sorry— I couldn't help it. The Roosevelts and many of America's leaders were of this stock. . . . My wife was born and reared in Kentucky. She is of English ancestry—but I hope you will not hold that against her."

Mr. Vosburgh then expressed his regrets that he had not been more specific in his previous letter concerning his church affiliations.

"Is church membership a requirement of your clientele?" he wrote. "Since you did put the question—it might be well for you to tell me which ones are on the approved list. We go to various churches—but as I stated in my last letter—we do not now belong to any particular one. We like some

better than others though—so if you will tell me the ones
that are on the approved or disapproved list I can tell better
whether we should be compatible with your group."

Mr. Vosburgh was by this time slightly exhausted and more
than slightly disgusted by the situation in which the Inn's
management had placed him.

"Well, this is quite an ordeal to have to go through in an
effort to get a room for ten days," he concluded in his letter.
"Maybe it will be worth it—I don't know. Anyway, whether
I win or not, the account of the effort will be one well worthy
of a place in my history book."

In reply to this letter, the management of the Inn informed
Mr. Vosburgh that there was no space for the period he requested, and recommended that he write away for accommodations to "other very attractive" resorts in the Phoenix
area.

Mr. Vosburgh answered, expressing his surprise that the
hotel was canceling his tentative reservation while the details
were being completed.

"Now if it be true that you are not trying to discriminate
against us, suppose we talk about another period for our
reservation. I find that some friends of ours, Mr. and Mrs.
H. W. Hill, are planning to be there for a period of two or
three weeks commencing January 25th."

Mr. Hill had completed all his arrangements for staying
at the Inn. He was at the point of forwarding his $150 de-
posit when he learned of the hotel's rejection of Mr. Vosburgh's request for accommodations. Mr. Hill immediately
wrote to Camelback, expressing his astonishment at the incident and asking the management for some clarification of
the situation concerning his friend.

"Now, I consider Mr. Vosburgh one of the finest men I
have ever known," Mr. Hill wrote, "one who is fully worthy
of any grade of hotel accommodations he might see fit to

request. It seems to me that your hotel has been most unjust and inconsiderate toward Mr. Vosburgh."

Mr. Hill added that he failed to see why the management of the hotel wanted specific information regarding Mr. Vosburgh's church and club affiliation and nationality, while in his own case it had not asked for this information.

"I feel sure you knew no more about me than you did about Mr. Vosburgh," he wrote. "This inconsistency and discrimination puzzles me. I might not feel as contented at a hotel where a good friend of mine was not also welcome—especially when he is of the high type of Mr. Vosburgh.

"Upon receipt of a satisfactory reply my deposit check will go forward to you."

The Inn's manager repled: "We didn't like Mr. Vosburgh's last letter, and did not feel we would be happy having him as our guest.

"You see, we operate a small family-type resort where personalities and their feelings toward us are important.

"In view of your letter, which, I very strongly feel, pries into something which doesn't concern you, we don't feel we would be happy having you at Camelback Inn either. Consequently, please keep holding your check for $150.00."

Upon receiving this letter, Mr. Hill commented: "From the tone of this letter, the Camelback Inn apparently needs a refresher course in public relations."

Mr. Hill's comment was one of many similar reactions to the attitude of the Camelback Inn. The one back in 1954, expressed by the National Association of Attorneys General, had become typical. That cancellation, and the many that followed, occurred because so large a number of people, informed of the prejudiced guest-admission policy, refused to use the resort's facilities. In the case of the attorneys general, a collateral question had been debated—the propriety of state officials, whose salaries are paid from taxpayers' money, using a racially discriminatory resort for an official meeting. But the principled issue was at the core of the community discussion. The public controversy itself was probably the reason that many business and other national associations followed suit; cancellations numbered in the dozens.

The Vosburgh incident and others, in some of which the ADL took an active interest, apparently caused the management to engage in some serious soul-searching. Instead of a course in public relations, Camelback decided upon a change of guest-admission practice; it manifestly preferred a democratic course of action to an undemocratic policy coated with genteel camouflage. On June 7, 1961, in a letter to the Anti-Defamation League which had sought clarification of the hotel's present policy, Jack Stewart, the Inn's manager, wrote:

"Religion is not and will not be the criterion for guest acceptance at Camelback Inn. I wish you would write me frankly in future, regarding any matters which might be remedied if some things occur which appear to be troublesome."

The Camelback Inn is today free of religious discrimination in its guest-admission policy.

How widespread *is* racial-religious discrimination? How important is it in the lives of those affected by it?

The conclusion reported in 1946 by psychologists G. W. Allport and B. M. Kramer may still be largely true. They said that it is a "safe estimate that at least four-fifths of the American population lead mental lives in which feelings of group hostility play an appreciable role."[19] We have already alluded in this book to the perverse consequences of this common affliction that vexes the mental lives of a large percentage of Americans—whether they are aware of it or not—the contradiction between the deep feelings associated with social discrimination (exhibited in prejudicial behavior), and simultaneous lip service to the "American Creed"—"You should

never judge a man by his race or religion." W. B. Brookhover and J. B. Holland describe the illogicality that flows from a deliberate concealment from oneself of the contradiction between public expressions and private behavior:

Our interviewers were constantly disturbed by the fact that respondents agreed with the "American Creed" almost without question, but at the same time agreed with all the unfavorable statements about minorities. The former (the interviewers) never reported, however, that any of the respondents were disturbed or even aware of this apparent discrepancy.[20]

How are we to account for this general ability to tolerate, without conscious questioning, two logically different sets of principles? It cannot be cynicism—otherwise the "American Creed" would not receive assent. The lack of awareness that anything is wrong affords one clue: the social discriminator does not think that exclusiveness in personal associations is at all reprehensible or contrary to the "American Creed." Typically, when the question is called to his attention, he indignantly asserts that everyone has the right to choose the people with whom he wants to associate—and that no one has the right to challenge it. This seems a fundamental truth, one so apparent that the large majority of Americans automatically resort to it.

It is human nature to select one's own friends. But in most people's minds there is a confusion of right and wrong in methods of selection. A choice on the basis of individual merit is one thing; selection on the basis of prejudice against entire groups is another matter.

The large percentage of Americans who have feelings of hostility to one group or another fail to make this distinction and deny that the principles of democracy or fair play are involved at all. This is an almost universal blindness, and it is evident that a fundamental impulse or a practice based on deep-rooted attitudes is at work.

Social-distance surveys offer us a key, because such surveys lead to the conclusion that personal association is the basic area, the floor of discrimination. When there is a conflict between powerful emotion and ideals, however lofty and sanctioned spiritually or religiously, conditioned emotions do not yield readily. In fact, those who are in their grip deny the fact of conflict or do not even recognize its existence.

Dr. Ruth Weintraub points out how the vigor of opposition to accepting personal associations with members of all groups compares with the strength of other forms of repugnance:

In order to test in some small way whether American practices and American attitudes were similar in the area of social discrimination, a series of doorstep interviews were secured, using as an approach the classic type of "social distance question," in which respondents were asked to name the "kinds of people they would prefer not to work side by side with, would prefer not to have live in their neighborhood, and would prefer not to entertain as a guest in their home." . . . The pattern was a remarkably consistent one. . . . Individuals discriminate the least in their working relationship and the most in their attitude on the neighborhood in which they wish to live.[21]

Because the feeling that underlies social discrimination as defined in this book is obviously stronger than the feeling behind other forms of discrimination, we should not be surprised to find it both pervasive and multifaceted; unfortunately, a "fateful progression" has been marked as well, a series of steps leading from mild social exclusion to harsh economic discrimination, eventually ending in violent political persecution.

From the point of view of social consequences much "polite prejudice" is harmless enough—being confined to idle chatter. But, unfortunately, the fateful progression is, in this century, growing in frequency. And as the people of the earth grow ever

more interdependent, they can tolerate less well the mounting friction.[22]

The memory of the Nazi atrocities of World War II thus makes it impossible to dismiss Jewish cemetery desecrations and swastikas scribbled on synagogues as merely evidence of juvenile delinquency or, at most, of crackpot anti-Semitism. There is a kinship among the vandalism of the German *Kristallnacht* before Christmas in 1938 and the synagogue vandalism in Germany on Christmas Eve in 1959 and the social segregation of Jewish groups in many countries of the world.

There is a tendency in the United States to discount social segregation as an isolated phenomenon. D. W. Brogan, an astute English observer of the American scene, has commented on the perceptible implications of such segregation for another religious and ethnic minority group in the United States—the Irish Catholics. His observations are relevant here:

From the political and social point of view, the Catholic program is one of segregation, voluntary or involuntary. It is to be seen in its most striking form in New England, especially around Boston where the Irish population, now settled . . . for a century or more, still carries a chip on its shoulder. . . . [This attitude] provokes hostile comment that recalls the atmosphere of a society in which anti-Semitism is beginning to be a real danger.[23]

These lines were written during World War II, when anti-Semitic demagoguery had been discredited in the United States by the war against Nazi Germany, the source of much of that demagoguery. Yet, to a shrewd observer from the outside, the climate of American opinion was still favorable to the progression from "segregation, voluntary or involuntary" that accompanies social discrimination to the "real danger" of anti-Semitism. What is the climate of opinion in the

1960s as revealed by current social practices? And what may we predict for the future?

The American people are extraordinarily fond of intimate groups. When Alexis de Tocqueville visited the United States more than a century ago, he noted an intriguing phenomenon which he described in a chapter headed "How the Principle of Equality Naturally Divides the Americans into a Multitude of Small Private Circles." De Tocqueville approved; there seemed to him nothing prejudicial about such a division of Americans—and in the 1830s, that was true.[24]

The situation has changed. Americans still love to form circles, but they tend to be neither small nor private: resort hotels, clubs, fraternal order chapters, veterans' posts. To avoid the charge of discrimination, commercial resort hotels masquerade as private clubs that may exclude "undesirables" by unwritten constitutions.

Social discrimination tends to pervade the one social group that is truly both small and private—the *clique*. To learn about discriminatory attitudes in the private lives of people in the United States, we must rely in large part on personal contacts or costly depth studies. Yet the data are essential because the clique is the most important area and source of social discrimination in this country. Vance Packard's parenthetical comment is pertinent:

In any community, the prevailing climate of segregation or intermingling is largely the total of what individual families are doing in their socializing.[25]

Ultimately, social discrimination rests upon the family, the basic unit of our society. Like all social institutions, the family is interested in the conditions of its own perpetuation —whom the children shall marry. According to some studies, this is primarily a matter of concern to the wife and mother,

and the wife's influence in restricting social intercourse between the family and other families from a different ethnic
background is significant:

In many communities, there is far more self-segregation of both
Gentiles and Jews at the wife level than at the husband level. Significantly it is the wife, rather than the husband, who makes most
of the social arrangements for a family. Dean found in his study
of Elmira, N.Y., Jews that the women were much more likely to
be self-segregating than their husbands. He found that only 12
per cent of the Jewish men confined their community activities to
purely Jewish organizations, 48 per cent of the wives did. Whatever the reasons for this greater isolation, it would indicate that
the wives have fewer personal, friendly contacts with Gentiles
than their husbands do.[26]

One obvious reason for the apparent difference in the
social habits of Jewish husbands and wives is that the men
have greater opportunities in their "business world" to become acquainted and friendly with non-Jews. However, the
hard fact remains that self-segregation is the other side of the
coin of externally imposed segregation. Although undesirable, turning one's back on one's neighbors is understandable
when the neighbors turn their own backs. What is surprising is not so much that almost half of the Jewish wives of
Elmira confined their community activities to purely Jewish
organizations, but that *more than* half were willing to participate in social activities with non-Jews—despite the frequent
rebuffs they might expect to encounter. And these rebuffs
are everywhere: not only in the home neighborhood, but
also when the Jew leaves home—in a vacation resort, a golf
club, a professional or school fraternity. This was confirmed
in 1955 in over-all surveys of social-discrimination practices
carried out in twenty-seven major cities of the United
States.[27]

That personal social contact has a wholesome influence is
proved by conditions to be found in many smaller com-

munities where Jews have a greater opportunity of meeting with their fellow citizens. Peter I. Rose studied such conditions in 175 towns of less than 10,000 in upper New York State. None had more than ten Jewish families. His researches bore out a long-established hypothesis that social contacts between members of minority and majority groups tend to reduce prejudice where those concerned enjoy equal status.

The most readily visible example of these exclusionary practices is the vacation resorts. At the same time, the resorts are the most vulnerable to criticism: whatever they may say, their chief purpose is not to provide accommodations and facilities for like-minded individuals to meet in friendship but to make profit for their owners. There have been several national studies attempted of the guest-admission policies of resort hotels and motels. One, carried out by the Anti-Defamation League in 1956–57, revealed that (among those on which information was available) almost one out of every four resort hotels was discriminating against Jews—and of those that might be considered nondiscriminatory on the basis of their publicly stated policy, one tenth had past records of discriminatory policies.

These findings are so striking that we quote at length:

In 1956–57, the League sought to determine guest admission policies concerning Jews of 3,014 resort hotels and motels located in the United States, Canada, Hawaii, Bermuda, Alaska, Puerto Rico, West Indies and the Virgin Islands. . . . It succeeded in obtaining information sufficient to evaluate about 35 per cent of them (1,065 hotels). Of this group, it found that a little more than 22 per cent (237 hotels) clearly discriminate against Jews. The balance, almost 78 per cent (828 hotels), it classed as non-discriminatory on the basis of their publicly stated policy. It must be noted that in this group of 828 non-discriminatory hotels appear 93 places (11 per cent) which, according to ADL records, have in the past given reason for belief that they discriminated against Jews. . . .

The ADL was unable to obtain adequate current information for 1,949 hotels, or almost 65 per cent. Many of the 1,949 hotels consist of establishments that have consistently declined to clarify questions that have been raised with respect to their policies toward Jewish guests. In fact, of the 1,949 hotels, 525 have previously come to the attention of ADL by way of complaints from the public, objectionable language in advertising and promotional literature, etc. The group, representing as it does 27 per cent of the hotels about which ADL did not obtain current adequate information, is significant. For it suggests ADL may be understating in its finding that about 22 per cent of the hotels about which it did get adequate current information are discriminatory. . . .

ADL obtained adequate current information for a fraction more than 34 per cent (933) of the 2,731 hotels in the United States. It found that almost 23 per cent (214 hotels) discriminate against Jews, while a little more than 77 per cent (719 hotels) declare a policy of non-discrimination. Again, ADL found that 11 per cent of the non-discriminatory group (81 hotels) have given serious cause for concern over the past few years in regard to their guest admission policies. And, of the 1,798 resorts about which ADL did not get current information, 505 were known to it previously for objectionable practices.

Two states, Arizona and Florida, have acquired reputations for attracting thousands of American tourists and vacationers to their hotels and motels. It is, therefore, significant to note that of the 214 American hotels which ADL found to be discriminatory, almost 39 per cent (83 hotels) are situated within these two states.

The situation in Arizona is far worse than in Florida. In Arizona, ADL found that nearly 45 per cent of the hotels it could evaluate bar Jews. By marked contrast, in Florida it found that only approximately 24 per cent (just slightly higher than the national average) discriminate. . . .

Our survey brought us information about the practices of 100 resorts in Michigan, Minnesota, and Wisconsin. Of this group,

34 per cent are discriminatory. For many years there has been widespread discrimination against Jewish vacationers by resorts in these three states. . . .

The findings in Canada revealed a somewhat worse situation than in the United States. Of the hotels about which ADL obtained adequate current information, it found that more than 28 per cent discriminate against Jews. In Mexico, on the other hand, only 3 per cent (one out of 31 resorts) were found to be discriminatory. Of 14 Hawaiian hotels surveyed, ADL found only one which bars Jews.

The report ends with a key paragraph:

The ADL survey observed that persons patronizing restrictive resorts are inclined to carry such undemocratic principles and practices into other aspects of their daily lives. Consequently, these may be responsible in part for some other un-American social patterns of discrimination.[28]

(The question has been raised by resort owners smarting under criticism: What of Jewish resorts which discriminate against Christians? The plain fact is that despite diligent efforts the Anti-Defamation League has never found that such resorts actually bar non-Jewish guests. They do advertise kosher cuisine, religious services, and the like, to convey to Orthodox Jews that they can visit the resort without violating their religious beliefs, but they do not explicitly bar their facilities to non-Jewish guests.)

In brief, about a quarter of the resort hotels and motels on which data were obtained excluded Jews from their facilities, although they were places of public accommodation, supposedly open to the public—and, in fact, legally obligated in many states to serve all patrons, regardless of race or religion.

A more difficult situation exists with regard to businessmen's and professional associations whose members meet for social purposes. When such groups practice anti-Semitism by excluding Jews from membership, they are often hard put to justify their position.

Thus far, the Merchants Club, as we have seen, has been able to walk the social-economic tightrope; for income-tax purposes it is a businessman's place of relaxation, but for other purposes it is a hail-fellow-well-met, no-Jews-wanted fraternity. What has been aptly said of the invidious distinctions practiced by certain resort hotels holds for this kind of hypocritical club:

The exclusiveness which has become the stock in trade of the resort hotels costs nothing and may enhance prestige. By advertising that it bars Jews, a hotel emphasizes the care with which it selects its clientele; the guest is honored by being accepted and feels a perceptible improvement in his social position.[29]

The so-called luncheon club is one kind of social structure, the resort is another. But there are still others, organizations that have some of the characteristics of both—plus additional ones of their own. Let's examine some of them in more detail.

CHAPTER 4. **The Public-Spirited Bigot**

•

The story of anti-Semitism in the Baltimore Shrine points up an aspect of human events that occurs all too frequently—the good deeds by men of good will frustrated by a handful of bigots.

In this case, the bigotry of a few caused not only the needless humiliation of a number of Jews but also marred the reputation of a fine national service society and broke up a long-standing cooperative effort on the part of several organizations to promote brotherhood.

Curiously enough, the sore of anti-Semitism that had been festering for a long time in the Baltimore Shrine came to a head as a result of a baseball game. This was, however, no ordinary baseball game; it was a popular annual civic event in Baltimore—the "interfaith baseball game" sponsored by the Knights of Columbus, B'nai B'rith, and the Baltimore Shrine. Each year it drew a capacity crowd to Memorial Stadium to watch the Baltimore Orioles play some other major-league baseball team, a great throng that came to enjoy a sports spectacle as part of a city-wide celebration of interfaith understanding.

For many years, this unique occasion set aside to do homage to intergroup fellowship stimulated the entire municipality: its business, civic, and religious leaders and its newspapers, radio, and television facilities cooperated.

The public and parochial schools of Baltimore were also brought into the picture. Schools with the best interfaith projects were presented suitable awards each year. Thousands of students were brought to the baseball game through what had become known as Operation Kid-lift. Blocks of tickets purchased by business houses and individuals were distributed free to the youngsters.

The day of the game was marked by much fanfare, including a formal luncheon—usually attended by the governor of Maryland, the mayor of Baltimore, the state's two U.S. senators, and other prominent leaders. In 1959, for example, more than 45,000 people saw Baltimore play Detroit. As usual, part of the game's proceeds was divided among the three sponsoring organizations for distribution to their respective charities.

Unlike the Shrine, both B'nai B'rith and the Knights of Columbus are frankly and avowedly religious organizations. The Shrine, however, a national fraternal organization made up of many local units such as the one in Baltimore, is nonsectarian. It is open to all qualified Masons—those who have attained the thirty-second degree through the Scottish Rite or the York Rite of Freemasonry. It is not an official Masonic organization and is regarded more or less as "the playground of Masonry." Its relationship to the Masons is somewhat comparable to the one that once existed between the 40 & 8 and the American Legion.

There is no restrictive religious policy in the national Shrine. Nor did the Baltimore order ever adopt any formal exclusion policy; none is enunciated in its bylaws. Nonetheless, Boumi Temple, as the Baltimore Shrine is called, operated from its inception seventy-five years ago under a tradition of discrimination against Jews.

Well-meaning Shrine members argued that there was no official policy of exclusion, that a few prejudiced individuals had succeeded in perpetuating their organization's religious barriers. They maintained that these individuals were beyond persuasion since they exercised their veto powers by blackballing in secret ballot and they thus remained anonymous. However, those who had consistently opposed the membership of Jews were generally known. They had revealed their identities in signed letters registering their objections to the placing of certain applicants on the election ballot. Top officers of the Shrine who received these signed objections could have, if they had chosen, brought some influence to bear to help correct an unfair discriminatory situation. The Baltimore Shrine's custom of barring Jews clearly had the tacit support of the rest of the membership.

It has long been a common Shrine custom throughout the country to permit members of one order to transfer to another through what is called a demit (transfer). The Baltimore Shrine, however, had adopted an equivocal attitude toward demits, correctly viewing their unrestricted use as a threat to its power to exclude Jews (who are accepted in the great majority of Shrines in the United States and in some of them occupy positions of highest importance). The Baltimore Shrine refused to grant transfers or recognize them from other Shrines in the case of Jewish members.

Instances in which demits from other Shrines were not given recognition began to reveal some of the cross-currents of Baltimore Shrine politics. One, for example, involved a young rabbi who had recently arrived from Pennsylvania, where he had enjoyed ten years of membership in a local

Shrine. With a duly acquired demit and instructions to contact the officers of the Baltimore order, he looked forward to a cordial reception by the Baltimore brethren. His expectations were heightened when he appeared as a guest preacher at a local church whose minister was active in the Baltimore Shrine. The minister was pleased to learn that the rabbi was seeking admission to the Shrine and offered to act as one of his sponsors.

The young rabbi met with the top officers of the Baltimore Shrine, an experience that proved a shock. Under a surface cordiality, he was advised not to seek to affiliate with the Baltimore order. The officers deplored the situation, stating that only a few men in their organization were opposed to Jews, but that the attitude of these few controlled the state of affairs, even though it did not reflect the feelings of the officers and membership as a whole.

The rabbi replied that his long association with the Shrine had been a pleasant experience and that he had enjoyed the fellowship of the Shrine and Masonic organizations. He refused to be deterred.

Later, he met the minister who had offered to sponsor his candidacy for membership and asked if he would still do so. The minister showed some embarrassment and finally advised him against affiliating with the Baltimore Shrine. But he suggested that the rabbi contact a certain former top Shrine official in Maryland, regarded at the time as one of the leading and most revered Masons in that area. Once a Potentate of the Baltimore Shrine, he now enjoyed the status of a kind of elder statesman.

The young rabbi did arrange a meeting with the former Shrine Potentate, who received him in his private office and greeted him most cordially. The Shrine leader made it quite clear that he thought Jews should be admitted to membership in Baltimore. He was reluctant, however, to sign the rabbi's petition for membership. He told the rabbi that he had signed several petitions for men and they had been rejected because they were Jewish. Therefore he was hesitant to add his name to another because it might do more harm than good. In these circumstances, the rabbi did not wish to press his case further.

Although this Masonic leader was a staunch adversary of the Baltimore Shrine's anti-Jewish discrimination and had spoken out against it time and again, he had long since given up hope of ending it.

This situation continued for some years. Jewish Masons in the Baltimore area were both kept out of the local Shrine and prevented from obtaining waivers so that they could become members elsewhere. Their ineligibility was complete and total until finally a change was wrought in this arbitrary behavior: The Baltimore Shrine at last began to grant individual waivers to Jews, who as a result were free to join some order outside of the jurisdiction of Boumi Temple. The interfaith baseball game had apparently had at least one tangible effect on the Baltimore order.

The question of B'nai B'rith association with the Baltimore Shrine had been a contentious one in the Baltimore Jewish community for a number of years. Many argued that the benefits derived from the association outweighed other considerations. They felt that the interfaith baseball game was producing a strong educational impact for the cause of good human relations, and that this ultimately would also have a salutary effect on the discriminatory Baltimore Shrine. But those who counseled patience began to find themselves a dwindling minority.

The issue started to simmer intensely in the fall of 1957, becoming an urgent problem in the Baltimore Jewish community. B'nai B'rith was now convinced that, despite the gains of the interfaith venture with the Shrine, the compromising position of the association demanded only one solution: the Shrine would have to discontinue its religious discrimination, or B'nai B'rith would have to sever its relations with the group.

B'nai B'rith leaders met in formal session with Shrine representatives and posed this issue in unmistakable terms. The response was unsatisfactory. There was no change in the position of the Shrine leaders, who declared that they could neither control nor bear responsibility for the actions of a minority within their midst.

There was one ray of hope left, a scheduled visit of George Stringfellow, then Imperial Potentate of the National Shrine. Many hoped that he might accomplish something constructive. He had the authority and prestige—if anyone did—to exercise a positive influence on the local Shrine. He had been seriously perturbed by the practices of Boumi Temple, which were having unpleasant and embarrassing repercussions outside Baltimore. Mr. Stringfellow arrived in Baltimore in December 1958 to see what he could do. His efforts were not successful.

The issue reached its climax in the summer of 1959. On July 14, the joint boards of the Baltimore B'nai B'rith lodges met in executive session, and voted to sever relations with Shrine sponsorship and to seek another group for continuing the interfaith baseball game.

On August 25, B'nai B'rith and the Baltimore Jewish Council held a meeting with the top officials of the Baltimore Shrine. A representative of the Knights of Columbus attended the session as an observer.

A B'nai B'rith spokesman opened the meeting by reviewing the history and purpose of the interfaith baseball game. He explained that over the years dissatisfaction within the Jewish community had steadily increased because of the sponsorship of the game by the Baltimore Shrine. He stressed the Shrine's lack of consistency in simultaneously practicing religious discrimination and sponsoring an interfaith event, adding that the purpose of this meeting was not to get Jews into the Baltimore Shrine, but to save the interfaith ball game. The Shrine's continued participation in the event, he said, was hypocritical and compromising.

The spokesman cited the Boumi Temple practice of sending emissaries to attend Masonic initiation ceremonies and distributing applications for membership to Christians only, slighting those of the Jewish faith. The Shrine officers exhibited no reaction to this charge. They made it quite clear that they felt their organization was a fine civic group and was not guilty of any wrongdoing. They saw no problem in continuing the joint sponsorship of the game and rejected the suggestion that they withdraw as a participant. They declared that the Shrine would not withdraw; if B'nai B'rith wished to do so, that was its privilege.

To resolve the impasse, the B'nai B'rith delegates suggested that the game be turned over to the National Conference of Christians and Jews. The Shriners were willing to include the Conference, but only on condition that the three present sponsors remain in the picture. This was rejected by B'nai B'rith, who decided to withdraw and so informed the Shrine in January 1960. Thereupon, Shrine leaders asked B'nai B'rith for a further conference. At this conference, Boumi leaders for the first time admitted that the Baltimore Shrine practice was wrong. They urged B'nai B'rith to continue as a sponsor of the ball game with the assurance that they would conduct an educational campaign within the Baltimore Shrine to rectify the situation. Thus assured, B'nai B'rith agreed to remain in.

Unfortunately, it was not long before it became clear that no real efforts were to be made in the direction of change. Accordingly, on November 23, 1960, B'nai B'rith voted to withdraw from the game and a month later served formal notice of its action upon the Knights of Columbus and the Boumi Temple.

There are a number of organizations in the United States that practice at least a subtle form of membership restriction. Many of these organizations have a reason for existence that is social in a broader sense of the word; they aim to serve the community, nation, humanity, or some other cause larger than the pleasure of their members. Known as service or fraternal organizations, they offer their members an opportunity to combine friendship with good deeds.

The *World Almanac,* limiting itself to relatively significant "associations and societies," publishes a selected list of about a thousand such groups, some with membership in the millions. The exclusion of Jews or other groups from certain of these organizations in which Americans come together for charitable, educational, and professional reasons is of the utmost importance on at least two counts: first, because they are not limited to any particular social-economic segment of the population; and second, because presumably the activity they engage in should be free to all prospective members willing to devote their efforts to a common worthwhile cause, be it assistance to delinquent children, provision of Thanksgiving dinners for the poor, attainment of higher professional standards for their members, or any other cause. Many of these eleemosynary associations do not permit Jews to join.

In 1956, an ADL study was made of the membership practices of the Benevolent and Protective Order of Elks. This fraternal and service organization, with a total membership throughout the country of more than one million, had branches in most of the states. The study covered 454 lodges in forty-three states of a total 1982 lodges in the nation. It was found that 64 of the lodges, or almost 15 per cent, did not admit Jews or made it difficult for them to become members. Specifically, 27 lodges did not admit Jews at all, and in 37 Jews obtained membership only with difficulty. On the other hand, there had been some improvement: it was ascertained that 24 of the lodges that presently admitted Jews had a past history of discrimination against them.

This exclusionary pattern was not restricted to any particular region of the country, although Jews in the United States are concentrated in the Northeast; it was nationwide. Jews were kept out of lodges in every national region; in the Northeast (in six states), in the North Central Region (seven states), South (three states), and West (seven states).

What great importance is it that one out of seven, or formerly one out of five, lodges of a national association with no remarkable social or economic prestige do not permit Jews to join, one may ask? The importance lies in the fact that one cannot shrug off the reaction against discriminatory practices in such middle-class-membership organizations as hysterical.

There is a certain superficial reasonableness in the argument that runs: Why raise all this fuss because a small group of upper-crust Jews are blackballed out of the "best" clubs —they can always join slightly less pretentious ones! *Must* young Jews get invitations to Junior League parties simply because they are well-bred and educated? Must a few Jewish children skate in the high-toned clubs or dance in the most fashionable schools? What if the woman's club that Mrs. Cohen cannot join, like the bridge club where she cannot play, excludes everyone who is not white, Anglo-Saxon, and Gentile? What if Mr. Cohen can't eat at his industry's luncheon club? He is apt, anyway, to be an independent entrepreneur dealing mostly with a Jewish clientele.

These arguments are often voiced, or at least thought. And some Americans are little enough interested in questions of principle when there are practical alternatives. Mrs. Cohen can play bridge at Hadassah or at the National Council of Jewish Women. There are plenty of plush hotels in Miami Beach and elsewhere to cater to Jews rejected by specific resorts.

But the exclusionary-membership practices of the national "service organization" destroy this line of defense for the *status quo*. The point about social discrimination is that it is contagious. It may begin at the upper rungs of the social ladder, but it works its way down and from one area of the country to another. Unfortunately, an invidious distinction is the easiest to adopt: human nature being what it is, people try to enhance their own self-esteem by denigrating others. This is by no means a universal pattern, but it is pervasive enough to merit concern. As Packard observes:

It is a nationwide phenomenon involving thousands of clubs. Some of the more elite New York clubs draw no line on religion at all; but in most American cities the line is quite firmly drawn. Atlanta is an example of a city where most of the country clubs and city clubs are either 100% Gentile or 100% Jewish.[30]

Whatever his income level, everyone wishes to distinguish himself. This is particularly true in a democratic society like the American, where there are no inherited marks of distinction in class, lineage, or style of living, where great masses of people share pretty much the same standard of living and material possessions.

There is a proliferation of clubs that attempt to achieve an alleged distinctiveness through selectivity of membership as well as of purpose. One cannot argue with a selectivity that is related to purpose: zoologists, for example, are entitled to enroll only persons professionally equipped to enhance the society's special purpose. But associations for general civic service may well be characterized as antisocial when they reject applicants on grounds other than that of character, fundamental decency, and the ability to perform the civic service.

In sum, the Packard status-seeker study suggests that not merely a few hundred or even a few thousand, but most of the five and a quarter million Jews in the United States are discriminated against. And with them, millions of other Americans are denied the right of free association with their Jewish fellow citizens. When service organizations restrict membership, Jews and non-Jews are kept from sharing socially useful work in a spirit of fellowship.

Discriminatory actions and attitudes of parents have an impact on the experiences and—consequently—the attitudes of their children. For instance, take the case of youth organizations that deliberately forswear exclusiveness because it is their purpose to live the ideals of American democracy. The Boy Scouts of America draws no color, nationality, or religious line; Scout leaders wish American children of all backgrounds to learn to play and work together. But throughout the country, entire neighborhoods are still segregated. As a result, some Scout troops, necessarily organized on a neighborhood basis, are automatically either completely white or completely Negro, completely Jewish or completely non-Jewish. The children, growing up with no equalitarian intergroup experiences, assume this exclusive pattern to be the natural one. And those of them who go on to college are ready for social discrimination there, too.

Segregation of Jews in college fraternities and sororities is part of the general pattern of discrimination in higher education, a subject we will examine later. At this point its existence should be mentioned, its relationship to a larger American pattern of social discrimination shown, and some statistics given.

In 1961, it was estimated that only two social fraternities out of the sixty-one national groups included in the National

Interfraternity Conference carried restrictive clauses in their constitutions. The abandonment of discriminatory clauses does not necessarily mean the abandonment of discrimination. Nevertheless, the proportion, roughly 3 per cent, is substantially lower than the 15 per cent of the surveyed lodges in the national service organization described above that barred Jewish applicants for membership. As noted, a slightly higher proportion of resort hotels studied in 1956–57 discriminated against Jews (22 per cent). And John P. Dean, in a study of discrimination against Jews in 248 American cities ranging in population from 10,000 to 500,000, reported the following findings. (Dr. Dean tested three areas of community life to measure the social acceptability of Jews: Junior League membership; country and city club membership; availability of homes in exclusive residential areas.) In one third of the 248 cities and in one half of the largest cities, all three areas were closed to Jews; twenty cities (mainly the smaller ones) accepted Jews in all three. In only one larger city were Jews acceptable in the three areas.[31]

Comparative statistics in this field cannot be regarded as definitive. But they do tend to indicate the varying intensity of social discrimination—depending on the situation, social-economic level, and age group involved—the influence and extent of exclusionary practices, and how these are related to certain conventional rationales.

Oscar Handlin has pointed out that historically social discrimination has "spread back from the resorts to the cities."[32] It also spread from the leisure-time, recreational, voluntary-service type of activity to the more serious problems that can be literally a matter of life and death. Between 1870 and 1920, as Handlin interprets the development, there was a change in popular American thinking about *private* and *public* institutionalized prejudice. Previously, Americans generally distinguished between social discrimination, which was felt to be an entirely private matter, and other forms of discrimination—in employment, education, housing, and public accommodations. The latter, it was felt, were fit subjects for public, governmental, and judicial control. But such protective legislation and its enforcement, it was held, should be limited to fields of public interest, which in this country traditionally did not include social discrimination.

Unfortunately, during the crucial half-century after the Civil War all organized prejudice, like social discrimination, came too often to be regarded as a private matter:

The means of exclusion were at hand through the development over several decades of the concept that large areas of social activity were private, in the sense that they were devoid of public interest and not subject to governmental interference. . . . Shortly after the turn of the nineteenth century, the pattern began to cover residential housing. In the rush away from the overcrowded central districts of the great cities, the desire for respectability was an important consideration. . . . Indeed, the scope of *private* seemed to widen steadily. By the second decade of the twentieth century it had already come to cover many forms of employment as well. After 1910, however, increasingly the Jews came to be discriminated against. . . . By the 1920's the *numerus clausus* had . . . found its way into . . . education. . . . Like a running sore, discrimination and exclusion had come to infect broad areas of American life. And the means of cure seemed limited indeed, for those areas had all come to be considered private, affected by and affecting no interests but those of the fortunate members of the association involved.[33]

During the past twenty-five to thirty years, governmental bodies have taken an increasingly active role in the workings of American society, and the scope of private interest has again been narrowed, that of public interest widened. In the depression-plagued 1930s, the New Deal intervened in the economic processes of the nation. It began by setting prices for consumer and producer, insuring collective bargaining for the benefit of labor, bolstering the farmer's position by underwriting his income, regulating the monetary agencies, and so forth.

The conviction that public bodies had a necessary interest in economic justice was followed by the conviction that economic discrimination against minority groups was contrary to that interest. This was felt most sharply during World War II, when the war effort required the fullest possible employment, and the exclusion of any group of Americans from employment opportunity was manifestly discriminatory and hurt the nation as a whole.

After the war, the concept of public interest was further expanded; discrimination in housing, education, and public accommodations gradually was officially recognized as detrimental to American society. There was greater awareness that minority groups could have no real equality of employment opportunity if they did not have free access to the schools that would train them for new occupations and homes situated in neighborhoods whose standards prepared their residents to make the fullest use of the schools.

Finally, it was urged, only if minority-group members could relax freely with other Americans in the public leisure-time accommodations would their standard of living rise sufficiently to allow them uninhibited access to the occupational, educational, and residential facilities of American society. A Negro who lived in a slum would receive poor early schooling and thus be educationally unprepared to enter an occupation. And, by extension, many suggested that a Jew who was refused accommodations in a public resort hotel was prevented from associating with the businessmen and professional people whose friendship was as necessary for his economic security and advancement as it was for the non-Jew's.

The economic disadvantage flowing from resort-hotel discrimination is, of course, only one small consequence of the evils that follow in the wake of such discrimination.

Social barriers, undemocratic attitudes, discriminatory criteria become imbedded as a result in general community custom. Hotel discrimination thus helps build into our culture practices toward Jews and others which relegate them to second-class citizenship.

In recognition of these truths, statutes were adopted in a number of states outlawing the right of resort hotels to bar guests on racial or religious grounds. These laws cover all public inns but not those establishments able to demonstrate their private-club character. In some resort communities, hotels still camouflage themselves as private clubs to escape the legal prohibition against religious and racial discrimination.

Another step is the removal of the barriers to freedom of association in areas that have been regarded by the defenders of the *status quo* as private beyond a shadow of a doubt. Discrimination in fraternal organizations is under attack—and, once again, the argument is an extension of the larger attack on discrimination as contrary to public interest. True fellowship is now recognized as essential to full education; college fraternities and sororities are clearly part of the larger academic scene. Learning takes place in a social framework of fellowship; when the framework differs for various groups of students, it does so at the expense of the university as a whole. In short, fraternities belong on the academic campus only if they are *con*fraternities, open to all.

We have moved away from the narrow concept that discrimination is important only if it affects the life-and-death needs of individuals, their bread-and-butter jobs. The problem now is to awake American public opinion to the fact that *all* racial and religious discrimination is a matter of public concern—and that, ultimately, social-minority-group discrimination in personal relations is the basis of all other forms of discrimination.

But there is a bedrock underneath that foundation: the strength of group feeling in the United States. Let us repeat that prejudice is the insistence on regarding individuals not as individuals but as group members—as group types, as stereotypes. How Americans feel about groups in general determines how they feel and act about individuals. This is by no means an exclusively American problem; a South African observer has noted the interrelation between group feeling and prejudice in his troubled country:

The greater and more intense the group feeling, that is, the stronger the identification between members of a group, the greater is the strength of the prejudice against the alien group and against those who are not members of one's own group.[34]

The United States is a country with many different groups, some clearly defined by race, others by religion—Negro, white, Protestant, Catholic, Jew. Other groups are less obviously distinguished, yet the distinctions as to place of ancestral origin or ethnic culture remain: Irish, German, English, Scotch, Italian, and—again—Jewish. Superficial observers may prefer to divide Americans according to their style of living into upper-, middle-, and lower-class groups, high-, low-, or middle-brow. But the average American, despite his official, public disclaimer ("only an American") still privately thinks of himself as a member of some ethnic-religious or racial group—Scotch Presbyterian, Irish Catholic, Reform Jew.

Cultural pluralists defend group loyalty; being proud of the values of one's own group need not necessarily mean rejecting the values of other groups. But the unhappy fact is that it has in the past resulted in conflict.

The recognition of group conflict in recent years has . . . led to a sense of crisis which must be evaluated against historical perspective. There is a strong tendency in American thought to ignore or minimize the very considerable amount of intranational group conflict which has appeared in various periods of our history. Yet an examination of the record will show that internal hostilities and disorders have been by no means infrequent.[35]

Unfortunately, group conflict is a fact of American life and part of our history. Group conflict is a factor behind social discrimination, as social discrimination is a factor behind all other forms of discrimination. Group conflict cannot be outlawed by decree; unthinking social prejudice cannot be removed by public legislation. Education is necessary—beginning with self-education.

II. DISCRIMINATION
IN HOUSING

CHAPTER 5. The Neighborhood

●

This is the story of Mrs. Jo Ellen Lobo, one of the millions of simple, decent people who quietly but determinedly live by a noble principle—respect for the dignity of others.

Mrs. Lobo—mother of four children and married to a Portuguese citizen employed as an economist with an international agency—first came to the attention of the Anti-Defamation League early in 1960, when she telephoned the League's Washington, D.C., office.

"Do you know the Sumner community just outside of Washington?" Mrs. Lobo asked, in a quiet but firm voice. "Last month we signed a contract to buy a home there, and the settlement is scheduled for next week. Now we've been told that we must sign a restrictive covenant. We simply won't do that. Can you help?"

The League did indeed know of Sumner, as well as its sister community—Spring Valley. Both are the creations of the W. C. and A. N. Miller Realty Company and are the most highly restricted neighborhoods in the Washington area. Without any attempt at subtlety, they are closed to "any person of the Semitic Race, blood or origin," including "Jews, Hebrews, Persians and Syrians."

The Millers insist that their customers accept this condition in writing on the face of the deed—although the signature has no legal force. They buttress their covenant with two other requirements: the Millers must approve new purchasers in their communities and they must be designated agents for the resale of the home. If the Millers don't approve, the banks don't lend mortgage money, the title companies don't insure title, and the agents don't sell.

The Millers have flagrantly flaunted their discrimination in order to create inflated values through synthetic exclusiveness. Moreover, they have brought to heel a number of influential persons in government service. Those who have signed covenants that will not permit their homes to be sold to or occupied by a Jew include a late justice of the Supreme Court, a former U.S. attorney general, three senators who have run for the Vice-Presidency, a minority leader of the House of Representatives, and a U.S. district judge.

The lamentable fact is that many of these influential and distinguished men who have allowed the Millers to hang their scalps in the trophy room of their real estate office did not necessarily approve the use of the covenant or share the Millers' anti-Semitism. A few have even denounced as un-American bigotry the covenants they signed. Others acquiesced without protest, apparently with the conscience-soothing rationalization that they were merely accommodating themselves to a necessary, if unpleasant, aspect of American life.

For years the Millers got away with it. Then they ran up against this uninfluential but determined woman who refused to compromise the principles by which she lived in order to gain material advantage.

The Lobos had a desperate housing situation. They had already sold their home, and unless they could get title to the

Sumner house, they would have to start looking all over again. With four small children to care for, this would be no easy task.

By Miller standards, the Lobos were eligible to buy a house in Sumner.

"We're Christian; we don't belong to any of the excluded groups," Mrs. Lobo told the ADL. "The problem is that we won't sign the covenant. We couldn't face ourselves or each other if we agreed to do so. We couldn't face our friends either, if we insulted them by putting our names to such a disgraceful paper. The people selling to us aren't happy about the covenant, and are willing to go ahead without the Millers' approval if they can. So are we."

The ADL was not surprised that the seller, too, did not care about the covenant. A sample poll taken in Spring Valley shortly before Mrs. Lobo's telephone call had revealed that a majority of its residents would have been just as willing to live there if there had been no covenant against Jews. Only 11 per cent said the covenant would have made a difference; no one said he would move away if the covenant were dropped. The inescapable conclusion was that the Millers were imposing their prejudice on a lot of people who had none of their own.

When the Millers heard that the Lobos were unhappy about the covenant, they asked them to come to the office, to see if the Lobos were really eligible after all.

"If the Millers want to approve us, let them come to see us," Mrs. Lobo told the ADL, adding that "even if we have to lose the house, my husband and I are determined not to sign such a covenant."

Mr. William Miller agreed to the meeting at the Lobos' home. He pointed with pride to the fact that many dignitaries had subscribed to the Miller plan. Didn't Mrs. Lobo want to join the ranks of the select? Mrs. Lobo was adamant: not that way, she didn't.

"I understand that some people who live in your communities haven't signed your covenant," she said.

"Those are just some very good friends whose beliefs I am sure of," Mr. Miller replied. "They are politicians, and it would be political suicide if they signed something like this."

"Since you have done this for some people for the sake of political expediency, won't you extend the same courtesy to me?" Mrs. Lobo asked. "It's against my principles to sign these papers."

"And it's against *my* principles to let you move in without my approval," he said. "In view of your ideas, I'm beginning to doubt whether you belong . . ."

Mrs. Lobo also was beginning to doubt that she belonged. She suggested that Miller write a letter disqualifying the Lobos as purchasers and return their deposit to them. This didn't appeal to Miller any more than signing the covenant appealed to Mrs. Lobo. Miller left.

A series of disquieting events followed.

First, Mrs. Lobo's own realty agent told her: "If you don't sign the covenant I don't know what's going to happen on the day of settlement. You'd better bring a lawyer."

Next, the president of the title company called. "I can sympathize with your objectives," he told her. "But I must tell you that if you don't sign the covenant I won't be able to give you clear title. I'll have to attach a rider excepting the covenants involved." Hesitantly, he added, "It would simplify things greatly if you would sign the covenant."

In the face of these events, Mrs. Lobo wondered if there was anything that could be done. The ADL told her that they had been fighting the use of covenants for many years, and that such restrictive covenants were not only offensive but were legally unenforceable. They further told her that the ADL believed that, on principle, the Lobos were entitled to clear title—unencumbered by dubious covenants—

and that it would try to find a title company that *would* give them a clear title.

The search for a company that would have the courage and moral stature to buck the Millers' power proved frustrating but educational.

One realtor told the ADL, "Why do they want to move to Sumner if they're not prepared to sign the covenant? I don't like the idea of anti-Jewish restrictions, but if a developer wants to run his community in a certain way, that's his prerogative."

The same attitude was shared by others, the League discovered.

It also discovered two influential realtors in Washington—Morris Cafritz and Abe Kay—who were not only sympathetic to the stand the Lobos were making but were also willing to help. Cafritz, who has an interest in the Lawyers Title Insurance Company, introduced the ADL to the president of the company. Lawyers Title agreed that the covenants in question were unenforceable. It said it would be willing to write clear title for the Lobos, providing it were indemnified against the legal fees involved in case of a nuisance suit brought by the Millers.

Lawyers Title then came up with a suggestion. Since the business had been offered to another title company first, it felt that precedent value would be stronger if that company wrote the policy on the same conditions Lawyers Title was offering. This would give more impressive notice to the real estate community in Washington that at last the Millers' policy of discrimination through the use of restrictive covenants was being challenged. The suggestion was transmitted to the first title company.

On the morning of settlement day—scheduled for four o'clock that afternoon—there were still many loose ends. Although the sellers, on the advice of their counsel, expressed their willingness to sell without the Millers' approval, the matter of mortgage money was unsettled.

Mrs. Lobo called her grandmother in California and told her of her predicament.

"Jo Ellen, don't sign those covenants," her grandmother said emphatically. "They're against every principle this country was built on. I'll send you the extra money you need to buy the house free and clear."

The first title company was still making up its mind. At 10 A.M. its representatives arrived at the ADL office. Couldn't the ADL understand that the company was in business, that it was not a crusader?

The ADL said that it was not interested in quixotic crusades, that what it was proposing was realistic, ethical business procedure.

This conference ended inconclusively at noon.

At 2 P.M. the title company's counsel called the ADL.

"We will give the Lobos clear title insurance if the ADL will provide counsel in the event of a nuisance suit."

The favorable decision was telephoned to Mrs. Lobo.

"Do you mean that I can have the house and that I won't have to sign the covenant?" Mrs. Lobo asked.

"Yes."

"I was prepared to sacrifice our deposit," she revealed. "Our lawyer friends advised us it was hopeless to challenge the Millers. But you did it, and you won."

"That's kind of you to say so," the ADL representative replied. "But *you* did it."

Although the closing that afternoon was conducted in a businesslike manner, everyone in the room felt he had participated in a tense struggle. The exhilarating sense of accomplishment, victory, good will was inescapable. When the last account was struck and the last signature written, photographs were taken of the president of the title company standing between buyer and seller. The seller embraced Mrs. Lobo and wished her well.

Mrs. Lobo had her house. Far more important, though, she had not compromised the principle she lived by—respect for the dignity of others.

Self-education begins at home, in the home, using *home* in its concrete as well as metaphorical sense—the house where one lives as well as the family itself. We have already pointed out that bread-and-butter discrimination has its origin in the attitudes and practices fostered by discrimination in personal, private relations, or what is called "social discrimination." And in speaking of the Boy Scouts, we noted how children are deprived of the opportunity to practice democracy in their social relations by the homogeneity of American neighborhoods. The Scouts, many of whose troops are all-white or all-Gentile, sometimes assume such composition is the pattern of friendship associations—particularly since their parents also associate almost completely with neighbors of their own color or ethnic background.

Obviously then, social discrimination practiced in leisure-time activities is almost inevitable because of the absence of opportunities for routine daily contact at home with persons outside one's own special group. Or to put it another way, since the neighborhood group is restricted—or restricts itself—along certain lines, those who are excluded from the neighborhood *become* outsiders, regardless of whether they are such by any objective criteria.

The falseness of the rationalizations justifying residential discrimination become most evident in the cases of famous nonwhites who have been denied homes in neighborhoods where they would be more than welcome if they were white. Olympic star Dr. Sammy Lee, a war hero of Korean extraction; and Jackie Robinson and Willie Mays, the Negro baseball stars, would have been perfectly acceptable in the neighborhoods that rejected them if their potential neighbors had been willing to accept them simply on their own merits. But these celebrities became dramatic instances of the blind prejudice that is the wellspring of housing discrimination.

How damaging segregation practices in residential neighborhoods can become for the national welfare was highlighted when it became known that Ralph Bunche had refused an important post in the State Department rather than subject his family to the inhibitions of life in a Negro ghetto in the nation's capital. Lee, Robinson, Mays, and Bunche are outstanding Americans who have managed through superlative gifts of mind or spirit to overcome the obstacles that discrimination places in the paths of nonwhite citizens. But for many millions of their fellows who are less gifted, the scarcity of opportunities at the very threshold of society—*at home*—is a powerful economic and social deterrent. Residential discrimination reinforces the minority status in employment and education that American nonwhites—Negroes, Mexicans, Orientals, Puerto Ricans—inherit.

In this respect, the Jews in the United States do not suffer so profoundly or so widely as the nonwhite minority groups. For the nonwhites, virtually any kind of housing is a tremendous problem; they simply cannot find adequate homes in sufficient numbers to meet their living needs and are forced to live in slum areas. American Jews are not underprivileged on this score. Whatever their financial bracket, they are able to find homes in every part of the country that meet their *material* circumstances.

But American Jews have only limited access to homes in some of the neighborhoods that conform to their *social* aspirations. One might say that Dr. Bunche's predicament is more typical of an American Jew than of an American Negro. Only the exceptional Negro like Dr. Bunche faces the problem that the American Jew typically faces, of being able to live comfortably within his income—or beyond it if he wishes—but he cannot live everywhere. There are neighborhoods, as we have seen in the case of Mrs. Lobo, sprinkled throughout the United States in which Jews are unwelcome as either tenants *or* home-owners.

Housing discrimination limits nonwhites to a few neighborhoods. For them, the problem of widening the areas of residence is the vital one, since it has been clearly established that better neighborhoods foster higher cultural and social standards.

For American Jews, housing discrimination produces only slight economic consequences. It is of concern, however, because of the social and psychological consequences that follow in the wake of segregated neighborhoods. Unlike the nonwhite, the American Jew finds segregated neighborhoods no bar to his economic progress. Rather, he is concerned because discrimination in housing, like social discrimination, is a threat to the Jewish status.

A fact of American social life—perhaps an unfortunate one, but one that cannot be ignored—is that where a person lives is frequently indicative of where he stands on the ladder of social values. Our society has often been pictured as mobile and dynamic; so it is. Here, as perhaps nowhere else in the world, an individual can move up or down the social structure, taking his family and associates with him, in the course of a decade or less. American social status tends to be fluid and not inherited, as it traditionally has been in Europe. Yet, it is still considered necessary to make that status, newly gained or retained, discernible to others. This is defined in terms of residence and neighborhood as well as of private associations. People share their social status with their compeers—with those who frequently live in the same neighborhood and who belong mostly to the same clubs.

It is on this point that the indignation of American Jews

parallels the bitterness of the nonwhites. Although American Jews suffer many fewer indignities, they are equally outraged by the abrogation of the principle of fair and decent human relations. Nonwhites resent the barrier that discrimination in housing raises against their advancement in American society; American Jews resent the withholding of recognition of their group advancement.

Among Jews, this discrimination causes significant psychological distress. All over the American landscape, American Jews perceive pockets of residential segregation—neighborhoods into which they cannot gain access. If this is typical of American group life, and if the suffering of nonwhites is admittedly greater than theirs, why are American Jews disturbed? Is this still another example of their oft-remarked hypersensitivity to fancied slights?

Perhaps Jews *are* more sensitive than other groups to the implications of segregation. After all, they still remember the centuries-long European ghettos and Pales of Settlement where their forebears were confined, resulting in their disastrous alienation from the rest of Western society. And they most vividly recall the still-fresh memory of the most recent ghettos, which the Nazis reconstituted in some of the most civilized cities of eastern Europe—Warsaw and Bialystok, for example—as a prelude to the physical extermination of six million European Jews. These are historic facts that still live in the thoughts of American Jews and cannot be shrugged off as paranoia.

American Jews have learned a bitter lesson from the history of their people—a lesson they see being repeated in the prejudicial treatment of minority groups less fortunate than they in the United States. Any group that is isolated from the mainstream of a national society, whatever the pretext, must be prepared in such times of stress or emergency as war or depression to bear the onus of popular anger at the frustrations that accompany the period of strain. Considering the natural human urge to find a scapegoat in times of distress, perhaps such ugly occurrences as the race riots in Detroit in the forties and the anti-Semitic demagoguery of a Father Coughlin in the thirties could not have been prevented. But certainly they would have assumed less frightening proportions were there not still so large a distance separating Negroes from many whites and many Jews from many Gentiles. This "social distance" is perpetuated by lack of the personal, everyday contact that comes with living in the same neighborhoods.

⎩American Jews cannot accept the claim that segregation in housing is simply a typical expression of American group life. It is not democratic. According to American principle, all men are entitled to live wherever they wish, if they meet certain economic—not *political, racial,* or *religious*—qualifications. ⎭

Let us take a look at American history in an attempt to answer this fundamental question: *Is segregation of neighborhoods for different groups part and parcel of American life?* Has it always been present? If not, when did it arise? Under what circumstances? And under what circumstances may we hope to see housing discrimination end? What is the present situation? And what can we see for the future?

In the first two centuries of the history of our country, roughly from the middle of the seventeenth to the middle of the nineteenth century, residential neighborhoods did not reflect social status to the extent they do now. Housing was closely tied to the opportunity for the ownership of land on which the homes could be built. The early colonists did indeed bring over the European system of latifundia—the Crown deeded large estates to members of the nobility or to commercial bodies (such as the Dutch West Indian Trading Company) for purposes of development. But these estates quickly began to break up with the colonization of the New

World by pioneers who vigorously asserted their own land claims.

Within a century, when the newly independent states organized to form a "more perfect union," a number of states issued specific declarations banning monopoly of land. Universal access to land meant universal access to housing. That principle was expanded to the nation as a whole in the Fourteenth Amendment to the federal Constitution and in an accompanying statute which declared, "All citizens of the United States shall have the same right, in every State and Territory, as is enjoyed by white citizens thereof to inherit, purchase, lease, sell, hold, and convey real and personal property."

It was in this spirit of the common right to equal access to land that during the first century of the Republic the federal government parceled out the free territories on a first-come, first-served basis. The abuses that flowed from unscrupulous land agents and speculators are notorious. But oddly enough, the profit motive, even when it employed chicanery and sometimes violence, still proved an equalizing factor in the distribution of land.

In those early days of American history, then, individuals could gain possession of land on which they might build homes; the only consideration for the sale was financial. No regard was paid to the caste or ancestry or religion or ethnic identification of the would-be buyer. There was much corruption and profiteering on a vast scale as individuals strove to exploit the riches that lay in the earth. But invidious prestige was never at stake. There was no dead hand of restrictive covenants on real property, to insure that it would be bought and sold only by those whose ancestors had come over on the *Mayflower,* or who were the "proper" color, or who had some similar artificial claim to distinction. The proper party in real estate dealings meant in those days only the one who would pay or sell for the right price.

Later, government found it necessary under pressure of public opinion to curtail many of the practices of the land speculators as contrary to the public interest. Though the government's actions may have been high-handed, its appropriation and distribution of land was essentially not discriminatory against minority groups. This nonrestrictive, objective attitude was a common one toward land and housing —characteristic of American economic and social life as a whole.

The new American took a dispassionate view of land as property. To some individuals, the ownership of "the good earth" undoubtedly continued to represent—as it did elsewhere in the preindustrial world—a classic way of life. In their view, land was meant to be accumulated, to be held in tenure, to be transmitted from generation to generation as the one perfect *real* estate.

But for the new American, such property had no metaphysical or ideal character, any more than did a horse or cow. Land—including the house on it—was a commodity like any other and, like all commodities, could be held, bought, or sold as a matter of individual choice. No American felt bound by extrinsic considerations of prestige or status to retain the land in his possession past the period of its usefulness to him. He could not restrict the purchaser of his land from reselling it to whomever he pleased. He could not determine who should be permitted to gain possession of his neighbor's land—any more than his neighbor could tell him who should gain possession of *his*.

All this was taken for granted. It was part of the laissez-faire, strongly individualistic common sense that was so typically American. Historians and sociologists agree that the American character has not basically changed; we have remained pragmatic, opportunistic, basically unsentimental in our attitude to land and home. Americans tend not to be deeply attached to any single local habitation. Their forefathers crossed oceans to establish new homes; their fathers moved in vast numbers from farms to cities, from the East to the West. Now, for the ordinary American a home remains a building where he lives for the time being, not an essential part of his total life, as it has been in other countries and times.

Statistics bear this out. The average American family moves once every five years, principally for economic reasons—a better job or an opportunity elsewhere.

For this reason, the contemporary limitation on the right of some Americans to change their address runs counter to the American privilege of moving freely. When limitations of residence deliberately restrict members of minority groups as a group, the nation as a whole is being restricted.

The restrictions on residence as we know them started in the middle of the nineteenth century, when industrialization began to change the face of America. (As already noted, social discrimination began to be practiced openly during that same period—another confirmation of the connection between living location and associates in "home" activities.) For two centuries, hardy Americans had been inching westward in search of fortune and security in the free lands; now the movement took on large-scale proportions.

Unlike the earlier migrations, the new industrial migration represented a concentration of population rather than a dispersal. Large numbers of workers moved from the relatively open spaces of the country to the more crowded cities, where the new factories were located, and in previously rural areas citylike organisms sprang up around mining sites. The migrants all required homes near their place of work. The native-born workers found themselves in competition for residences not only with one another but also with the flood of alien immigrants attracted to the same parts of the country for the same or similar jobs.

The largest number of immigrants in the country's history disembarked on American shores during this period. Between 1870 and 1920, about twenty million new Americans arrived—from Italy, Hungary, Russia, Japan, Greece. At this time, too, the United States really developed into a nation of minorities. The Negro minority, now free, was joined by new immigrants of various ethnic origins and religions.

The tensions created by the competition for jobs, homes, and education led to a new stratification among the minorities. The Negroes—the largest and most conspicuous group, with a recent history of exploitation and cultural depression —were relegated to the lowest rung on the status ladder. The immigrant minorities were evaluated in terms of their conformity to the prevalent American population patterns of national, ethnic, and religious background. White, Protestant, Anglo-Saxon, West European were favored over Negro, Jewish, East European Slavic, or Mediterranean.

Despite the bias against both the old "native" and the new "foreign" minorities, both economic and social discrimination remained localized. The kind of housing segregation we are familiar with today did not develop until the end of the 1870s. Like Negroes and Catholics, Jewish minority-group members were kept out of certain trades and occupations. However, virtually none of these minorities was compelled to reside in certain areas and kept out of others. Many of the minority groups, both the established and the new ones, *voluntarily* formed compact communities—generally in the poorer sections of the growing cities, since their income was low. Besides, they were more comfortable living with their own people in a familiar culture reference.

As the nineteenth century drew to a close, exclusion by means of such devices as zoning became the rule in many areas of the nation. The tremendous population increase and movement had brought with it sharp competition for sites and housing. The 1880 census recorded 50,155,783 inhabitants of the United States; by 1920, the figure had more than doubled, to 105,710,620. One fifth of this increase was due to new immigration; to the older residents of already populated areas, *all* the newcomers, whether migrants from rural areas or new arrivals on American shores, represented a threat to their stability. They seized on the newcomers' superficial "difference"—color, language, religion, not basic human qualities—as pretexts for excluding them from their neighborhoods. By doing so, the old-timers hoped to remain secure during this time of turmoil from a feared decline in their own living standards and changes in their accustomed manner of life.

At first glance, this fear would seem unjustified. There is more than enough land in the United States to house vast numbers of people. In fact, it has been estimated that America has enough room to house the entire present population of about 180,000,000 at a density of twelve families to the acre within part of a single large state. But this statistic is deceptive because it is predicated on a kind of rural economy, one far less centralized than the industrial society Americans have been living in for the past century.

In order to operate, our modern technological society requires the concentration of millions of individuals within small areas. Factory and office workers need homes near their places of employment. Even with excellent roads and the widespread ownership of automobiles, it is impractical for the vast majority of Americans to live more than fifteen or twenty miles from their places of employment. It is within this twenty-mile radius of the metropolis proper or at least in the larger metropolitan area that the most desirable homes are situated. Here, land available for residence and offering access to the necessary utilities, transportation, shopping, and other facilities is at a premium. It is here, too, that we now find, after two centuries of relatively open occupancy, widespread discrimination and segregation in living accommodations during this third century of American history.

Briefly, these are the circumstances under which certain elements in American society—those who believe they have a prior claim to tenancy and those who control the construction of new housing—have imposed their own standards of fitness on minority purchasers. Broadly speaking, the discriminatory elements fall into two categories—official and unofficial, public and private. But in practice, as we shall see later, the categories merge; the various agents that keep alive discrimination in housing complement and reinforce one another—the present land- and home-owners, the builders, the brokers, the banks, even the interested government agencies.

At a quick glance, there seems to be a consensus favoring minority discrimination in housing. It would seem as though all elements in our society are lending their support, not merely their tacit assent, to the proposition that some Americans are more deserving than others of exclusive housing or housing in more desirable neighborhoods. How else can we account for the continued matter-of-course signing of racially and religiously restrictive clauses in new housing contracts. Such covenants have been declared legally unenforceable by the Supreme Court; yet they are not illegal as contracts, and many persons using them seem to prefer to disregard the spirit if not the letter of the law.

In many cities there has been an increase in residential cooperatives during recent years. One might think a liberal attitude would prevail in this expression of the American spirit of mutual aid. Yet many of these cooperatives surreptitiously or openly limit their membership to "Christians only."

Finally, there are the local government bodies, sworn to defend the civil rights of all inhabitants of the community.

Many of these actively abet some individuals in their determination to keep others from living in their neighborhoods. Municipal and county authorities pass and administer zoning ordinances designed to exclude certain groups from residential opportunities; they exercise their administrative powers in a variety of ways, sometimes overtly and sometimes covertly, to exclude "undesirables."

Faced with these practices, one tends to throw up one's hands, assuming pessimistically that they can't be altered because exclusiveness is integral to American mores—irrational, widely accepted, a part of the American psychology and group relations. Logically, these questions come to mind: If Americans as a nation, and as individuals, did not strongly believe that housing discrimination was justified, would they permit it? Would purchasers of homes sign restrictive covenants if they were not in favor of them? Would citizens' groups press local government units to legislate insidious zoning regulations? Would builders, brokers, banks, and even federal agencies write this bias into the terms of contracts, loans, and insurance if they were not sure of the "voice of the people"?

Yet there is firm ground for believing pessimism to be unwarranted, for concluding that the organized housing institutions have misread the actual wishes of the American people. Bias in housing, besides being a relative latecomer to America, does not currently reflect popular sentiment and it is *practically* as well as morally wrong.

In May 1959, the attitudes of residents of Spring Valley, Maryland, a restricted community near Washington, D.C., were surveyed by the Anti-Defamation League. This is the community contiguous to the Sumner area where Mrs. Lobo made and won her fight.

This key question was asked: *If there had been no covenant against Jews, would you have been willing to buy a house* [in Spring Valley]? Fifty-eight per cent of those queried said they would have been willing, and only 11 per cent said they would not. Fifteen per cent were undecided and 15 per cent refused to comment.

This further question was asked: *If restrictive practices against Jews were removed, would you move from Spring Valley?* None of those polled said yes.

These are practical, although "iffy," questions; the replies are practical ones. The Spring Valley residents signed restrictive covenants when they bought their homes, but the covenants were not viewed as essential to their purchase. From their replies, the residents seem to consider the covenants quite incidental. In fact, they seem to consider them with complete indifference.

It might be said that the Spring Valley results are atypical, since the metropolitan region surrounding the nation's capital is a special community with relatively high cultural, educational, and—perhaps—moral standards. The nation as a whole, it may be argued, really supports restrictive covenants.

But a month before this, in April 1959, a study by the Gallup organization of a representative cross section of the American people yielded similar data corroborating the Spring Valley findings. One of the questions was: *Suppose a Jewish family were going to move in next door to you. Would you say you would not like that at all, that you would not like it but it would not matter too much, or that it would not make any difference to you?*

In reply, 86 per cent of the white Christians polled said that a Jewish family moving in next door would make no difference to them; only 2 per cent said they would not like it at all. ADL questioned high school students about the acceptability of Jews as neighbors—with slightly less favorable results. Perhaps the somewhat different response came because ADL's question was more affirmative than the one used by Gallup. When asked to reply to the question *I would like to have* [Jews] *in my neighborhood,* 18 per cent strongly agreed, 45 per cent agreed, 21 per cent were uncertain, 9 per cent disagreed, and 4 per cent strongly disagreed. In short, 84 per cent of the high school youth surveyed would not definitely reject Jews as neighbors.

This is a comparatively healthy attitude—healthy in comparison to the almost universal acquiescence to restrictive covenants. Does this mean that Americans do not really believe in the reasons for the exclusion that is so widely practiced? Apparently they do not. The same national Gallup poll asked for comment on a provocative statement typical of the usual justification for housing restrictions: *The trouble with letting Jews into a nice neighborhood is that sooner or later they spoil it for other people.*

Only 2 per cent of the white Christians who answered agreed strongly with this sentiment; 63 per cent disagreed, either strongly or mildly. Apparently the real estate interests that press for continued prejudice against Jews in housing are mistaken when they insist that they are merely carrying out the wishes of their non-Jewish clients.

The popular disagreement with the complaint that Jewish neighbors spoil nice neighborhoods is interesting; even more instructive perhaps is the extent to which so many of the respondents were *uncertain* as to whether they agreed or disagreed with the complaint. As many as 26 per cent of the respondents, more than a fourth of them, said they were not sure whether it was true or not that Jews brought deterioration to neighborhoods.

Here, then, is the nub of this aspect of the problem: an honest confusion as to the facts. On the one hand, people have been subjected to a constant stream of statements averring that exclusion of neighbors "undesirable" for racial or religious reasons is absolutely necessary for "neighborhood values." On the other hand, they know it is "wrong"—undemocratic, unethical. But perhaps they think residential segregation is not so widespread for Jews, after all.

•

This happened to Joe Gratz, co-owner of radio station KBON in Omaha, Nebraska (population 400,000). It could have happened—and does—in any of a number of other cities in the United States.

Joe Gratz got married, and, like newlyweds everywhere, he and his bride began searching for a place to live. After a great deal of looking, they found one that appealed to them —on South 36th Street in Omaha. There were the right number of rooms; the neighborhood was to their liking; the rent was within their budget.

The agent for the apartment house was the Stuht-Bedford Realty Company. Mr. Stuht, who showed them the apartment, told the Gratzes that in his opinion they were a most desirable prospective tenant and that the apartment was theirs subject to confirmation by the owner, Jack O'Keefe, who was then on a visit to Florida.

Mr. Stuht telephoned Mr. O'Keefe. The owner's reaction both shocked and dismayed Mr. Stuht.

"I won't approve Gratz as a tenant," Mr. O'Keefe said, in substance, "because he's a Jew."

Mr. Stuht passed on the owner's reaction to the Gratzes. "I'm unhappy about this, but, in view of Mr. O'Keefe's definite turndown, there is nothing I can do," he told them.

He was wrong. He did do something. After Mr. O'Keefe turned down two subsequent prospective tenants because they were Jewish, Mr. Stuht canceled his management of the O'Keefe property.

The Gratz–Stuht–O'Keefe case was one of several of a similar nature that had come to the attention of the Anti-Defamation League in Omaha. As a result, on April 14, 1959, the League sent this letter to Mr. Herbert L. Osborne, president of the Omaha Real Estate Board, requesting the board's assistance in eliminating religious discrimination in apartment-house rentals:

During the past two years, a growing number of cases have been brought to the attention of the Anti-Defamation League. The authenticity of each of these cases has been verified through interviews with the applicant, the owner, or, most frequently, the real estate agency. In almost all of these cases, a real estate agency, managing a property on behalf of a prejudiced owner, has been involved in denying a rental unit in an apartment house to members of the Jewish faith. Most of the realtors involved have been frank in admitting the validity of the complaint. They have stated that such acts of religious discrimination were personally distasteful; nevertheless, they have added that the agency was helpless in the face of the owner's instructions.

One local agency, which recently dropped an account rather than continue a party to discrimination, has earned the respect of all fair-minded, decent citizens. However, other agencies have shrugged off any responsibility, claiming it would not be wise to antagonize their clients, and pointing out that there is no assurance that another agency would not accept the account in the event they chose to discontinue it. At the same time, real estate agencies, handling discriminatory accounts, have been concerned lest their own reputation for fairness be injured. . . .

We believe that an agency which participated in an act of religious prejudice, even at the request of the owner, is a party to an immoral act.

Therefore, we appeal to the Omaha Real Estate Board to initiate an educational program directed at owners. We would also suggest that a voluntary pledge be made on the part of all real estate management firms to refrain from handling accounts which would involve them in acts of religious discrimination. Such an agreement on the part of all agencies would prevent loss of income to anyone.

We are certain that members of the Omaha Real Estate Board are ethical people, concerned with the welfare of Omaha, and the professional reputation of realtors. In addition, we are certain that voluntary action by the Omaha Real Estate Board would be equally effective as legislation such as has been passed recently in Colorado, New Jersey, and New York, preventing discrimination in private housing.

Two days later the Omaha Real Estate Board took up the matter of religious discrimination at its meeting. What resulted was an unequivocal and enlightened stand on the matter:

The Board of Directors affirms as the policy of the association that religious beliefs of renters or purchasers can have no importance or bearing as to their suitability as tenants, owners, or neighbors. Listings which seek to exclude members of any religious faith involve the Realtor in a prejudicial act which runs counter to America's belief in religious liberty and full respect for each man's faith.

Realtors should seek to convince owners, renters and others who seek to impose such religious limitations, of the unethical quality of such a request; and, failing the elimination of such restrictions or request, refuse to serve as agent in the sale, management, or rental of such restricted properties.

We take this action in order that the reputation of the Realtors as professionals, seeking to serve the community and its welfare, remain inviolate.

A random survey that the Anti-Defamation League made in 1958—with no claim of completeness—confirmed the existence in more than a dozen metropolitan areas of neighborhoods that ban Jews. These areas were located on the East and the West coasts, in the South, the Midwest—in short, all over the country. The fact that the neighborhoods were in metropolitan areas is of utmost importance to American Jews, essentially an urban group, as well as a very mobile one because this means that they are unable to move in complete freedom from one city area to another.

Some 40 per cent—more than two million—of America's Jewish citizens live within the environs of New York City. In New York City proper, the most desirable new housing for prospering families are the cooperatively owned luxury apartments. Yet, the League reported, of 175 such cooperative buildings studied, about one third had no Jewish tenants. In the city's suburbs, some of the more desirable districts kept out Jewish residents. Bronxville, in Westchester County, was the most notable example of a deliberate and constant effort to maintain a *Judenrein* community.

Metropolitan Chicago, the fourth largest Jewish population center in the United States (282,000), contained a number of suburban residential communities that had erected barriers to keep Jews out. This situation was particularly distressing in the North Shore suburbs. There has been a very substantial increase in the Jewish population of the North Shore in recent years but some of the most attractive North Shore communities almost entirely excluded Jewish residents.

Let us here scotch a common misconception. It is simply not true that only wealthy Jews are discriminated against in housing, any more than it is true that only wealthy Jews are the ones to be blackballed from private associations with non-Jews. The same discrimination occurred in many areas of Chicago and its suburbs, and at almost every economic level.

(This is not to say metropolitan Chicago Jews have been forced to live in slum sections. They can and do obtain housing in almost every part of the Chicago area at a level consonant with their economic position. But there are specific pockets of metropolitan Chicago where Jews cannot live. This is the disconcerting reality.

The same pattern appeared in other large city areas where Jews are concentrated. Let us look at the cities with Jewish communities of over 50,000—the dividing line between a large and a medium-sized Jewish community in the United States. Philadelphia, with about 331,000 Jews, has seen some recent improvement; Jews are now able to live in areas where they could not live before World War II. But in nearby Baltimore (80,000), the residential restrictions have been so rigid that even third- and fourth-generation Jews whose families have been in Baltimore for more than a hundred years have moved into all-Jewish suburbs—the new Jewish and non-Jewish neighborhoods in Baltimore automatically dividing into distinct areas.

In Cleveland (88,000), Jews have been virtually barred from certain suburbs, and a visible pattern of higher-class Jewish "ghettos" has begun to appear in the new fashionable areas. San Francisco (55,000) is reputedly a conspicuous exception to residential restriction on Jews. But Los Angeles, with a far larger Jewish population (the second largest in the country, with 390,000), is well known for its walls against freedom of residence for all minority groups, including Jews.

Nor are the cities with medium-sized Jewish populations (between 10,000 and 50,000) an exception to the general discriminatory rule in housing. The ADL's 1958 survey yielded an impressive list of places in which it was then virtually impossible for Jews to live where they wished. Each represented a suburban as well as an urban area because the pattern of residential segregation for Jews rapidly spread from the core city to the marginal suburban areas. Cities are becoming inhabited by the upper and lower class; the middle class, to which Jews overwhelmingly belong, has been moving to the suburbs.

This middle-class move to the suburbs, originally the home of the wealthy and the poor, began during the twenty-five years preceding the end of World War II. During that period (1920 to 1945), no less than 75 per cent of the new developments for owner-occupancy were built in the peripheral sections of cities. During that same period many of the patterns of middle-class residential segregation of Jews in the suburbs were established.

However, the Jews did not begin to move into the suburbs in large numbers until after World War II. When they did so, they found that the pattern to put them "in their place" had already been set. In a sense, this was the crucial period. In the decade after World War II, well over nine million additional residents moved into suburban counties. Or, to bring the figure up to the 60s, the Census Bureau reported in January 1960 that the suburbs had accounted for most of the population increase since the 1950 census. The nation's population had increased by 16 per cent between April 1950 and April 1959. Of a gain of 24 million, the suburbs had accounted for 15 million. The 168 metropolitan areas had showed a nine-year population increase of 19 per cent; but the central cities in these areas had increased their populations by only 1.5 per cent, while the suburbs reported a 44-per-cent gain.

Given the generally high economic status of the Jewish population of the United States, one might assume that Jews were becoming home-owners to a greater extent than non-Jews. But studies of home ownership conducted in 1941,

1950, and 1955 showed that this was not the case. Seven out of ten white Catholic and Protestant families in the medium-sized communities examined owned their own homes; only one half of the Jewish families did so.[36]

Perhaps this was due to a developmental lag. The fact that Jews are traditionally city-dwellers, and city-dwellers tend to rent rather than buy homes, may have caused the Jews to lag behind other similar middle-class groups in home ownership. Certainly, the younger Jews were exceeding their parents as home-owners, and the next generation will in all likelihood catch up with the national pattern. These studies indicate that more than 44 per cent of the Jews living in certain communities own their homes, compared with the national average of 51 per cent.

But where are these homes to be located? Are they sprinkled haphazardly throughout suburban areas or are they being sealed off within unseen neighborhood walls?

CHAPTER 7.   **Suburbia**

●

More than three hundred years ago the English poet John Donne observed: "No man is an island, entire of itself; every man is a piece of the continent; a part of the main. . . ." This also applies to communities.

Yet in the five fashionable communities that comprise Grosse Pointe—suburbs of Detroit—some persons believed their area could indeed be an island unto itself. And on this island, they believed, they could devise a special kind of yardstick to measure the worth of human beings. If one fit the measure—and one could afford it—he and his wife and his bairns would be allowed to buy a house in Grosse Pointe and live with the "best" people, who were, of course, those of Grosse Pointe; if not, they had the freedom to live elsewhere.

A most logical, fair, and democratic arrangement, or so it appeared to the Grosse Pointe Property Owners Association, who dreamed up and operated the most elaborate—and original—method this side of heaven for measuring the worth of man.

With the efficiency of a well-oiled business operation, the

wealthy and powerful elite of Detroit who lived here had successfully protected the "exclusivity" of their community from
"undesirables." For some time their screening method received no publicity, no adverse criticism. Then, early in 1959,
rumors began circulating that a private detective, an English-
man, was policing the sale of Grosse Pointe property. The
rumors brought into focus, in the spring of 1960, a civil suit
in which John A. Maxwell, a former resident of Grosse
Pointe, sought the recovery of property that was being held
under lien by Grosse Pointe Properties, Inc. Maxwell also
sought to dissolve an agreement with the defendant that gave
the corporation power to screen prospective buyers of the
unfinished Maxwell mansion in Grosse Pointe Park. In addition to Grosse Pointe Properties, Inc., the defendants in the
suit were the Grosse Pointe Property Owners Association;
Grosse Pointe Brokers Association; Maxon Brothers, Inc., a
realty firm; Paul Maxon, the firm's president; H. Gordon
Wood, an attorney; Incorporated Properties, Inc.; Paul R. O.
Marden; and the National Bank of Detroit.

The private eye turned out to be Paul Marden, a former
executive secretary of the Association, who, by the time of
the suit, had been succeeded by Orville F. Sherwood. Under
questioning by Maxwell's attorney, the ingenious "point
system" of measuring a man and his family was unabashedly
explained by Sherwood, and the "score card" the Association
and its race- and religion-conscious allies used to grade a
prospective buyer was made an exhibit in the case.

As Sherwood explained it, here's how the system worked:

After a prospective buyer's name was submitted by a real
estate broker to the Association, it engaged a private detective to fill out the questionnaire. The completed report was
then turned over by the Association to a committee of brokers, who added up the scored points and sent it back to headquarters. The Association then made the final decision—

whether or not the prospective buyer had made a passing grade.

Of utmost significance was the fact that passing grades were based upon a sliding scale. Sherwood testified that of the maximum possible 100 points, Poles would pass with 55 points, Southern Europeans with 75, Jews with 85. Negroes and Orientals had no passing grade; they were automatically disqualified.

"A person with a very swarthy complexion would probably get a low rating," said Sherwood.

The rating sheet—a masterpiece of amateur sociology, racism, and cynical snobbism—that was filled out by the Association's hawkshaw was two pages long and divided into four alphabetical categories with notations of the maximum point potential.

Section A was headed: "Is Family American? Americanized?" and then listed eight questions. Copied verbatim from the rating sheet, proudly headed GROSSE POINTE PROPERTY OWNERS ASSOCIATION, these questions were:

(1) What descent. Mr.?_____ Mrs.?_____ 7

(2) American Born. Mr.?_____ Mrs.?_____ 7
    If not, how long in U.S.A.? Mr.?_____ Mrs.?_____

(3) Is way of living American?_____ 4
    (A) What is his occupation?_____
        Typical of his own race?_____
    (B) Are his friends predominantly American   14
        or otherwise? _____
        Specify type_____

(4) Appearance: 6
    Mr. Swarthy Very__Medium__Slightly__Not at all__
    Mrs. Swarthy Very__Medium__Slightly__Not at all__

(5) Accent: 6
    Mr. Pronounced__Medium__Slight__None__
    Mrs. Pronounced__Medium__Slight__None__

(6) Names typically American? Mr._____ Mrs._____ 3
    Typical of own race?   Mr._____ Mrs._____

(7) Ages and number of persons in family_____ 3

The first section of this document accounted for 50 of the possible 100 points. Question 8 had a marginal instruction for the investigator: "Do *not* grade this question."

(8) What persons (if any) other than the subject and children:
    (A) Occupy present residence?
    (B) Will occupy future residence?

Following these eight questions was a "Note to executive secretary's office":

> If there are to be occupants in new home other than subject and his children, *and if subject passes,* complete additional reports should be secured on other occupants.

Section B, which began page 2, was headed: "General Standing," contained six questions, and accounted for the remaining 50 points.

(1)   20
    (A) If in a company, what is his position as distinguished from his occupation? (As given in A–3A above)_____
    (B) How does above position and type of occupation stand in public estimation?
        High__Medium__Poor__
        NOTE: A station in life of sufficient eminence could be capable of producing a passing grade despite all other considerations in this report

_____

(2) Have his dealings been considered reputable?_____ 8

(3) How has his family been thought of in previous neigh- 8
    borhoods:
        Highly?__ Medium?__ Of bad repute?__

(4) How is present home kept up?   5
     Exterior and grounds?_____ Interior?_____

(5) Dress: 4
         Mr.   Neat_____ Slovenly_____
         Mrs. Neat_____ Slovenly_____
         Mr.   Conservative_____ Flashy_____
         Mrs. Conservative_____ Flashy_____

(6) General Education: 5
         Mr.   Good____ Fair____ Poor____
         Mrs. Good____ Fair____ Poor____

Section C was headed "Additional Information," and asked these questions:

Religion: Mr._____ Mrs._____
Grammar: Mr. Good_____ Fair_____ Poor_____
           Mrs. Good_____ Fair_____ Poor_____
Military Service, if any:_____

Section D was headed "Narrative," and had a space in which the Association obviously desired further enlightening comments on the prospective buyer's Americanism, dress, grammar, complexion, and choice of religion.

Another form—a "Blue Form"—was used specifically for scoring prospective Jewish buyers. As far as was known it did not have a Star of David on it, nor did it suggest that a Jew wear one on his sleeve should he somehow manage to survive the test and be permitted to live there.

This "Blue Form" was introduced by the brokers' screening committee. Although not many Jews at any time had attempted to purchase Grosse Pointe property, the screening committee felt obliged to make sure only a few—the "best" Jews—would enter the exclusive, predominantly white, Anglo-Saxon, Gentile Grosse Pointe heaven.

The "Blue Form" asked the same questions but allowed fewer points for the same "achievements." For instance, the scoring on the "Blue Form" would have conservative dress count three points instead of four, and a good education would give a Jew a maximum of four points instead of five.

When Sherwood was asked to testify what would happen if a seller did not concur with a rejection decision, he revealed that he would personally go to the property-owner and try to persuade him to comply. He also revealed that a broker who violated the rules would lose his commission.

Another defendant, Paul Maxon, president of Maxon Brothers Realty and secretary of the Association, noted in a pretrial deposition that the Association had a right to prevent a broker from selling to a prospect it believed could hurt property values. Property values, he explained, could be hurt by Negroes, Southern Europeans, Italians, Syrians, and Armenians.

The Maxwell case made headlines from Detroit to Hong Kong. Individual citizens, the newspapers, and organizations fighting anti-Semitism fired broadsides of criticism. The Michigan Attorney General and the Corporation and Securities Commission instituted a public hearing on these screening practices. Subpoenas were issued to the officers and members of the board of the property-owners' and brokers' associations and the officers of Grosse Pointe Properties, Inc. The hearings were to determine whether or not the use of the questionnaire and the point system was in violation of Michigan law or the Michigan state constitution.

Attorney General Adams stated that, at the very least, these practices were "morally corrupt." Governor G. Mennen Williams, himself a registered voter in Grosse Pointe Farms, condemned the screening as "an odious situation."

A letter mailed to Attorney General Adams by Dr. Jean Braxton Rosenbaum of Detroit, when he learned that an investigation was planned, said:

My dealings were with Mrs. Irene Bledsoe and Mr. DeSantis of Johnstone & Johnstone, Grosse Pointe. When I asked to make a bid on a house, I was told by Mr. DeSantis that I must await being passed by the Grosse Pointe Property Owners Association. This took several weeks. I was told then by Mrs. Bledsoe that I could not buy or even look at a house in Grosse Pointe because I was Jewish and could not qualify. I will not belabor the point with needless detail, but I think some details of personal biography might be of interest in the light of my being disqualified.

First of all, I am half Jewish and my wife is not Jewish at all. I was told by Mr. DeSantis, incidentally, that she qualified and could move to Grosse Pointe. I forgot to ask them about my two-year-old son. We are all native-born citizens, light complexioned and without accent. My wife is a scholarship alumna of Cranbrook Academy. The half lineage which is not Jewish in myself is from my mother. She is a Braxton. She's a direct descendant of Carter Braxton who signed the Declaration of Independence. I was raised in Detroit and am a *cum laude* graduate of Wayne University. I am the inventor of the artificial electrical heart and have contributed this invention without recompense to the community. I am a member of Sigma Xi, the national honorary research society. I am the author of many scientific articles in Medicine and am honored to be the recipient of four national medical awards. I am Instructor at Wayne State University College of Medicine for which I accept no salary. . . . I hope my personal experience can be of some use to you. . . . I could go on but I think my point is clear. . . .

According to the rulers of Grosse Pointe, Dr. Rosenbaum did not measure up to elite standards. Yet in the Detroit *Free Press,* R. Noble Wetherbee, an attorney and secretary for the Grosse Pointe Property Owners Association, defended the screening system by saying:

> The form contains a note, "a station in life of sufficient eminence could be capable of producing a passing grade despite all other considerations in this report."
> For example, if Einstein had wanted to move here he would have passed even if he didn't make the points.

Without leaning on Einstein for support, the two associations, in a joint statement given the *Free Press,* described the point system as merely an effort to maintain real estate values and that the point system had been misunderstood: "These values are a matter of supply and demand. When a house hunter learns that a cliquish or clannish group of families, unlikely to absorb local customs, and against which some general prejudice exists, has begun buying in a certain neighborhood, this house hunter tends to look elsewhere where he believes his investments will be more secure. Even the unprejudiced person is affected. It works in vicious circles—fears of lowered values, lower values because of lower demands—appraisal matter."

This masterpiece of economic theory and entrenched interest concluded that "the system would seem to be the most careful and considerate method possible for making the best of a difficult fact—of prejudices which affect real estate values, just as street paving and water systems are also facts affecting value."

Burying its righteous corporate head in the golden ground of Grosse Pointe, the two associations apparently cared little about the adverse world-wide publicity its actions aroused.

Congressman Charles Diggs, of Detroit, traveling at the time in Asia and Africa, found that the image of America had been damaged. The Detroit *News* reported: "Diggs said the Grosse Pointe area residential screening story broke in the papers of Hong Kong and Tokyo while he was there, 'putting us on the defensive.' "

At home, the Reverend Arnold Johnson, a Congregational minister, said in his sermon that Jesus Christ "would have failed the test," for Christ would have been obliged to answer "carpenter and itinerant preacher" to the question on occupation, and to the query on friends, "mostly Jews, some Greeks, and sinners."

In Michigan, after prolonged hearings, state officials issued a ruling ordering the associations to drop the system.

On August 20, 1960, *The New York Times* reported: "A property owners association and a real estate brokers group in the exclusive Grosse Pointe Suburbs east of Detroit have agreed to abandon their point rating system for screening prospective home buyers.

"The elimination of the widely publicized procedure was interpreted in the Michigan Attorney General's office as a major step in the state's drive against discrimination in real estate."

However, on January 17, 1961, a Detroit *Free Press* headline read: REAL ESTATE SALESMAN TESTIFIES GP [GROSSE POINTE] STILL USES SCREENING, COURT TOLD.

Communities that would be islands unto themselves don't give up their splendid isolation so easily. Neither state rulings nor public outrage nor common decency nor danger to the American image seem to be more important than property values.

An ironic postscript may be added to the Grosse Pointe story. On October 18, 1961, many months after the incidents just recounted, David Brinkley, the NBC-TV commentator, offered an interesting program about gangsters. Brinkley established that professional hoodlums frequently live in the nicest homes of the best neighborhoods across the nation. As he exhibited pictures of several palatial estates, he asked his audience rhetorically whether it believed gangsters necessarily end up lying dead in the streets or in jail. Answering his own question, he went on to say (names and addresses deleted):

Well, the truth is that most of them don't. Instead they wind up in places like these. Like Number _____ Road, Grosse Pointe, Michigan, the residence of _____ _____, described in the Senate as a major underworld figure. He is not in jail. He's here. [Photo of residence on camera] Grosse Pointe, a suburb of Detroit, is a leafy, pretty town filled with people of the most eminent respectability. But somehow it also includes a small colony of criminals, not only _____ _____ at Number _____ Road, but also _____ _____ at Number _____ Road, labeled on the record one of the biggest narcotics dealers in the country.

At Number _____ Road, Mr. _____ _____, whose record runs

to counterfeiting and narcotics. Moving on down, Number _____ Road was the home of Mr. _____ _____, also labeled in the Senate a major underworld figure. He died a natural death.

At Number _____ Road, Mr. _____ _____, who, the Narcotics Bureau says, is a prominent member of the Mafia. At Number _____ Road, Mr. _____ _____. Most of his police record was made during prohibition.

At Number _____ Road, Mr. _____ _____, arrested 15 times, served a little time for bribing a policeman.

Will the reader forgive us for wondering what were the passing grades attained by these citizens of Grosse Pointe?

We have mentioned various elements that foster discrimination and segregation in housing. They are all dominated by a very broad, very loose, and essentially very false single idea—the "harmonious neighborhood." *Homogeneity* is the slogan that unites home-owners, brokers, financial institutions, insurance companies, academicians, local and even federal agencies. The dream—or, more accurately, fantasy—is that neighborhoods should be all of a piece—racially, religiously, and economically. This fantasy has been impressed on the public by paid advertising in the mass-communication media, particularly magazines and newspapers.

The goal of a homogeneous neighborhood was originally pursued by the first large wave of settlers in the suburbs between the two world wars, many of whom fled the city to escape contact with minority groups. The suburbs were their Shangri-La. Naturally, suburban isolation could not last. Paradoxically, after World War II, the more successful minorities themselves joined the exodus from the crowded city. To them, the suburban style of life—based as it was on the independence of home ownership—became a symbol of Americanism. A second-generation Catholic, Jew, or Italian saw his "home in the country" as a sign of cultural acceptance; now he would become an authentic, middle-class American.

Thus, when he was denied the opportunity to buy a house in a particular neighborhood, he was deeply resentful. He felt that as a member of a minority group he was being rejected by American society. And so he was.

Why this rejection of minority-group members as neighbors? Some social psychologists trace it to a combination of two fears. The first is the social fear—the anxiety over loss of status if the neighborhood should be flooded by persons of "inferior" background. The second is the economic fear—that houses in the neighborhood invaded by the "outsiders" might lose their value as property.

There is also a third fear—popularly expressed as anxiety concerning the danger of intermarriage. If the children of the old-timers and the children of the newcomers play together, go to the same school, and become close friends, what is to prevent one of the "nice" children from wishing to marry the boy or girl next door, despite his or her "poor" background? In short, there will be a blurring of the group's identity, particularly if the newcomers differ markedly from the old-timers in race or religion.

Apprehensive that these fears—connected with status, money, and group identity—may be realized, the established home-owners accept (and sometimes are induced to press for) a pattern of one-type occupancy in their residential areas. Assuming that the would-be neighbors are attacking their "values," the established home-owners and tenants put up a wall of contract, agitation, and—if need be—violence in "self-defense." For help they call upon powerful allies who possess an imposing array of weapons calculated to beat off the "attacks" of the minority groups.

Spokesmen for the building industry usually disclaim responsibility for discriminatory practices in selling or renting homes. They assert that they are forced to go along with the prejudices of their clients. The general public insists on segregated housing, they say, and builders cannot be expected to go contrary to the wishes of the largest part of their market for the sake of a smaller part. They are bound by the imperatives of profit and loss.

Their plaint is only partly true. The whole truth requires that builders admit that they often lead rather than follow the public in housing discrimination, and that they possess more rather than less power than the general public to change the situation. Often, when they have been pressed, they have changed. Until 1950, the official code of ethics of the National Association of Real Estate Boards stated:

A realtor should never be instrumental in introducing into a neighborhood a character of property or occupancy, members of any race or nationality, or any individual whose presence will clearly be detrimental to property values in the neighborhood.

But in 1950, under public and private pressure, this rule was amended. The references to "detrimental" races, nationalities, and individuals were deleted, and the sentence rephrased to conclude: ". . . a character of property or use which will clearly be detrimental to property values in the neighborhood."

Despite this deletion of a statement offensive to minority groups, the fact remains that most real estate people have not altered their basic beliefs. On September 14, 1961, Connecticut's Commission on Civil Rights opened a hearing in the upper-middle-class city of Greenwich. The complainant was the Commission itself and the basis for the hearing was the following letter on the stationery of a Mrs. Olive Braden, a Greenwich real estate broker:

OLIVE BRADEN ASSOCIATES   July 1, 1961
ALL SALES PEOPLE:

From this date on when anyone telephones us in answer to an ad in any newspaper and their name is, or appears to be Jewish, do not meet them anywhere!

If it happens on Sunday tell them we do not show on Sunday, take a phone number and then throw it away!

If they walk into the office in answer to an ad we are running, screen them carefully. Here are some suggestions if you are uncertain about their nationality:

1. What is your church or school preference?
   (If they have none)
2. Are you Christian or Catholic?
   (If they are neither)
3. And if you are still in doubt, find out what they want to look at, the price, etc. etc. converse at length with them, and if you are still in doubt, show them ONE house—just one, and tell them if something comes in that we can show them we will call them.

This will give us time to check on them here in the office, and either clear them or forget them.

We can do only one thing by cooperating with them and that is be liable to severe criticism by the Board and our fellow brokers, as these people are everywhere and just roam from one broker to another hoping to get into Greenwich.

Please digest this carefully and be guided accordingly.

(sgd.) *Olive*

OB/cc

Mrs. Braden, whose agency is a member of the Greenwich Real Estate Board, admitted writing the memo to her sales staff. But, she explained under oath, she had done so as a result of criticism by members of the Greenwich Real Estate Board, leveled at her because she had sold homes to Jews. (Reports had been current for years that Jews encountered special difficulties when they sought to find homes in Greenwich.)

Mrs. Braden's testimony raised the question whether the Greenwich Real Estate Board had participated in a conspiracy to prevent Jews from buying property in the area. However, the case was closed with the issuance of a cease and desist order to Mrs. Braden. The question whether the Board itself was guilty of a concerted attempt to prevent Jews from purchasing property in Greenwich has yet to be probed.

The Greenwich real estate situation may seem extreme, but with respect to suburbia it is probably typical. The fundamental fact is that the majority of real estate people still believe in a kind of Gresham's Law of Neighborhoods. Their theory is that just as bad dollars drive out good ones and thus lower the value of currency as a whole, so "bad" residents (those from the wrong side of the tracks) drive out "good" ones (those with the proper background), and thus depress neighborhood values. This theory obviously encourages exclusionary practices.

O. G. Powell of Des Moines, Iowa, who retired as president of the National Association of Real Estate Boards on November 15, 1961, looks upon government efforts to eliminate discrimination in housing as a "perversion of the traditional and constitutional rights of the American citizen in its most vicious form." Public housing, he says, acts "to destroy communities, miscegenate races, regiment society, perpetuate poverty and thwart enterprise." Urban renewal projects, in his view, "serve to relocate slums rather than to eradicate them." Leaving office, he called for a crusade on the movement to end racial discrimination in housing. Mr. Powell merely verbalized for his fellow realtors at the National Association annual meeting the policy followed by most real estate boards—open opposition to antidiscrimination court decisions or legislation. For example, after the U.S. Supreme Court rendered its 1948 decision in the case of *Shelley* v. *Kraemer* declaring racially and religiously restrictive covenants unenforceable in court, the Los Angeles Real Estate Board urged a constitutional amendment to reverse the Supreme Court decision.

Generally speaking, wherever there is no state or city law prohibiting racial, religious, or ethnic segregation, the vast majority of private builders, following the dictates of their own prejudice, maintain a strict exclusionary policy. They do so both individually and collectively. On many occasions, both the National Association of Real Estate Boards and the National Association of Home Builders have urged members of their groups to use "protective covenants" to safeguard the individual home-buyer. However, the individual home-buyer often hesitates to protest a neighbor's infraction of one of these covenants and thereby refutes the righteous cry of the builders that they are simply obeying the *vox populi* of the prejudiced home-owner or tenant.

This protestation of righteousness is further belied by the sanctions that real estate boards have been known to impose on builders who, even unwittingly, commit infractions of the one-type neighborhood dictum. For example, in a village near Houston, Texas, a builder and real estate agent who joined in selling a home to a Jewish family were punished severely. The builder was not permitted to build any more homes in that village; the agent was refused property listings in the area. Such economic sanctions—or even the threat of them—are usually sufficient. Some liberal-minded builders believe themselves forced to put up all-Jewish or all-Gentile sections, and agents are careful to steer Jewish and Christian prospects to the appropriate area. This creates a *de facto* situation to which real estate people can point as evidence that Jews, as well as Christians, prefer to "stay with their own."

What is the position of the agencies that finance construction of homes—the various banks and lending institutions? Like the builders, most lenders are aware of the basic discrepancy between democratic ideals and the practices of preferential treatment given certain groups in loans for housing. The lenders insist that they make no racial or religious distinctions in their housing loans and point to substantial portfolios of loans to Jews. But disingenuously they fail to note that these loans are restricted to housing in certain neighborhoods; some banks and savings-and-loan associations frown upon loans to Jews for homes in "non-Jewish neighborhoods."

Fortunately, the Home Loan Bank Board, whose duty it has been to regulate the associations, finally adopted (in the fall of 1961) a policy resolution opposing racial and religious discrimination by the savings-and-loan associations under its supervision. This was the first such action by a federal agency charged with supervising mortgage-lending institutions. Sad to say, comparable agencies such as the Federal Reserve System and the Federal Deposit Insurance Corporation have not yet adopted a similar position.

The insurance companies bring up the rear. Pointing to the vandalism and arson that occasionally take place when the "wrong" people move into neighborhoods where the "right" people do not want them, they sometimes refuse to insure housing for minorities outside certain limited areas. The result is a vicious circle in which lender, government officials, and insurance men cite one another as authority: "the experts all agree. . . ."

The last—and perhaps most potent—authorities are the so-called intellectuals in the industry. If the exclusionist theories in housing originate with the builders, are accepted by the financial institutions, not rendered unlawful by the government, and assured by insurance companies, they are rationalized by the "academicians"—the professed intellectuals of housing. Many books on real estate practice do not merely describe the racial, religious, and ethnic minority problems; they justify the *status quo* as eminently reasonable. The National Association of Real Estate Boards, summing up its "educational" accomplishments, has asserted that there are 165 universities and colleges that offer courses in real estate, and in 40 of them, students can major in this subject. The NAREB happily points out that many of the texts used in these courses come from its own groups. The result? Thousands of brokers-to-be have been instructed in the Gresham's Law of Neighborhoods.

This theory of real estate—and incidentally of social—value is taught not only in schools and colleges, but is also incorporated in texts put out by reputable publishers and widely circulated in real estate magazines, newspapers, and home journals. As a result, builders and brokers who oppose the concept of the homogeneous neighborhood are regarded as troublemakers by some leaders in the real estate industry.

We have discussed so far only legitimate interest groups—those with an honest if misguided concern for the homogeneous neighborhood. But another real danger is represented by the out-and-out fanatical organizations that exploit the problem of equal housing for purposes of their own undemocratic agitation. These bigoted organizations operate on the periphery of neighborhood "betterment" associations, which they incite to direct action—and sometimes to violence—for the protection of their vested interests in a "pure" neighborhood.

It is interesting to note how groups of rabble-rousers, organizing *ad hoc* bodies, appropriate the high-sounding lingo of the Gresham's Law of Neighborhoods. Thus, one property-owner's association in the West campaigned for the

right of the American neighborhood to protect its own property values and to fix its own standards of culture, congeniality and happiness through its association. . . . Private property-owners living in the same neighborhood shall have the right to contract with each other concerning the occupancy of private housing accommodations in such area . . . and . . . they may form local associations for that purpose.

On the face of it, this statement on the right of a group of citizens to organize to protect its economic rights is quite innocuous. But things are not what they seem: the property-owners assert their intention to "contract with each other concerning the occupancy of private accommodations" with a view to maintaining, as they so vaguely and ambiguously phrase it, "standards of culture, congeniality and happiness." Since it is they who "fix" the standards, a potential property-owner in the area must live up to their standards or else he cannot live in the neighborhood.

Professional agitators exploit social anxieties for their hostile purposes, using the Gresham's Law of Neighborhoods as a weapon to justify separating one group of the population from all others. The result of this agitation, as we shall note, has been hostility, actively exploding into violence.

Violence is the ultimate, palpable danger of the pure-neighborhood concept. The homogeneous neighborhood cannot be accepted by "heterogeneous" minorities; they feel they have as much right to live where they wish as the "homogeneous" Americans have. When they assert that right and their assertion is restricted, conflict ensues.

The danger of violence for a stable and free society is obvious. What is less obvious is the source of this danger—the social mores that dictate where people may or may not live (if they are members of a minority) are truly injurious to individual civil freedom. Thus the problem is both social *and* political. As such, one would expect government to take an active role in resolving it. But government has not effectively committed itself to assuring the housing rights of individuals against social forces opposing the exercise of those rights. That is the political problem of our time in the area of housing.

The difficulty lies in the very nature of representative democratic government. Because it is extremely sensitive to public opinion, the government apparatus has tended in the past to give its consent to attitudes and practices of the American public that are only seemingly representative of democracy. During the 1930s, this country witnessed the introduction of a New Deal welfare economy the goal of which was to improve the lot of one third of a nation that, among other things, was ill-housed. The liberal New Deal agencies worked through private housing operations, which they implemented with public power and public credit. They worked pragmatically on the basis of how things were being done, rather than how they should be done, with the result that the federal government adopted and supported existing prejudices in the private-housing market. Prejudice in housing was thus given the invaluable assistance of the government's own covert coercive power.

This anomalous situation, which persisted from 1935 to 1950, meant that a democratic government was empowered to achieve a valuable social goal by sanctioning undemocratic theory and practice on a large scale. There was a formal policy change after 1950 as the government became aware that its position was politically untenable. Public opinion did not completely sanction segregation in housing. However, the practices of institutions traditionally lag behind their expressed ideals—the marks of prejudice are still discernible in the federal government's housing program.

The Federal Housing Authority was created under the National Housing Act of 1934 to encourage home-building and mortgage-lending. From the very beginning, the FHA accepted the same task the building industry did—protection of the "homogeneous" neighborhood. The FHA went so far as to send agents into the field to keep minorities from buying homes in "majority" neighborhoods and exerted pressure on builders and lenders neither to build nor to lend money to minorities for homes in the "wrong" neighborhoods.

The FHA's official manual explained: "If a neighborhood is to retain stability, it is necessary that properties shall continue to be occupied by the same social and racial classes."

This policy continued until several years after World War

II. Although the FHA now officially encourages open occupancy in housing developments that are publicly assisted, it does not attempt to control the discriminatory practices of private builders or lenders. The FHA system enables discriminatory builders to engage in real estate subdivisions without investing their own money, and at the same time it insures lenders against any loss on their mortgage loans.

The Home Loan Bank System has followed FHA practice and policy in encouraging—as well as respecting—segregation in private building. The Home Owners Loan Corporation went so far as to adopt a "neighborhood rating" procedure. What is a desirable neighborhood? The rating system tried to answer this question by breaking down the city or community into a number of homogeneous neighborhoods or areas. In rating populations, the inspector was required to list "foreign families" as well as Negroes. The foreign-born and the Negro neighborhoods were given a low rating.

Federal agencies, as already noted, are responsive to national opinion. When national minority-group organizations have pressed for revision of standards based upon antiminority prejudice, they have succeeded in effecting changes. It is clearly within the realm of possibility that a long step forward will be taken before this volume finds its way into the hands of readers. The federal Civil Rights Commission has urged the President to issue a federal directive which, with the stroke of his pen, will prohibit discrimination in any housing in our nation which is in any way directly or otherwise given federal financial assistance.

But most local governmental bodies—urban and suburban—are single-mindedly committed to preserving the *status quo* in their communities from encroachment by "outsiders." Consequently, local public agencies and officials have freely employed their discretionary powers over land use and building to prevent "detrimental" minority groups from entering "reserved" areas. Various administrative devices are at their disposal: they can file building violations; raise the assessed valuation of the property; disapprove plans or specifications; refuse arbitrarily to issue licenses; thwart or delay the completion of streets and the laying of sewer or water lines; refuse to interpret building requirements; and so on.

When their efforts at restriction or segregation of housing for different groups of the population are challenged by determined minority-group members or organizations, local government units have not hesitated to go to the courts to protect discriminatory housing as a thoroughly legal practice.

Finally, the courts themselves for some thirty years (1918 to 1948) sustained the constitutionality of restrictive covenants, despite the manifest damage to civil rights. During this period, the highest courts of fifteen states, the District of Columbia, and other regions all held these covenants to be both legal and enforceable. It is interesting to note that a federal court ruled (in a case involving Chinese in California)[37] that such discriminatory contracts were illegal. But in 1929, when the same issue came before the United States Supreme Court (in the case of *Corrigan* v. *Buckley*), it refused to make so clear-cut a finding. In fact, it implied its approval of restrictive covenants. Courts throughout the country followed the highest tribunal's lead, and American courts became instruments for the enforcement of oppressive private contracts in the area of housing. Property-owners who violated restrictive covenants were held in contempt or assessed damages.

In 1948, the Supreme Court finally prohibited the enforcement of restrictive covenants (in the case of *Shelley* v. *Kraemer*), but it did not state they could not be contracted. The inevitable result was the creation of numerous devices to accomplish the purpose of discrimination without running afoul of the letter of the Supreme Court's decision. The idea was to arrange for covenants that would not require judicial enforcement.

CHAPTER 8.   Exurbia

●

Heinz Pol, a writer, and his wife Ilse, unlike many members of their respective families, survived the gas chambers of the Nazis by escaping to the United States.

In July 1956, the Pols—who have a permanent residence in New York City—were looking for a country place when they came across Birch Groves on Candlewood Lake in the town of New Milford, Litchfield County, Connecticut.

It is a pleasant-looking exurban community, with some seventy homes, tennis courts, a beach, and other recreational facilities.

The Pols found a house to their liking and purchased it. Mr. Pol was told that operation of all the development's facilities—including its water supply and road maintenance —were controlled and administered by the Birch Groves Association.

"I was informed that all property-owners in the community were eligible for Association membership, and I promptly applied for admission—even before I moved in," Pol has recalled.

Within a few weeks after submitting his application, Pol received an answer from the Association. It was a brief note, signed by Forrest J. Spooner, the Association's secretary.

"The Board of Directors of the Birch Groves Association has fully considered your application for membership and I am sorry to have to report their decision to not approve such application."

There was no further explanation.

Deeply concerned, Pol tried to find out why he had been rejected.

"I was informed by at least three other members of the community that the reason I had been rejected was that I was of the Jewish faith."

Pol also discovered that a couple of Association members were Jews, but that they had been living in Birch Groves when the Association was founded in 1941 and had joined before the restrictive practice was introduced. Subsequent Jewish purchasers of Birch Groves property had all been rejected as members. The old-time Jewish neighbors assured him that newcomers were allowed to make use of the community water supply by paying a higher assessment than Association members.

The Pols liked their summer place so much that they spent the winter of 1956–57 there, and began to consider it their permanent home. Then, in May 1957, Mr. Pol received another letter from the Association's secretary. This one was a bit longer than the first letter and a great deal more disconcerting.

"We note that you are using our domestic water to supply your house at Birch Groves. You are not entitled to the use of our water and this is to advise you to arrange to discontinue its use. Unless you terminate this use within sixty days, we will be compelled to cut off our line at your property. . . ."

Pol checked his water taps to make sure that the Association hadn't advanced the deadline. The water was still flowing. Then he decided to check the facts.

He discovered that although the bylaws of the Birch Groves Association did not themselves carry discriminatory provisions, one section said that "the conditions of the sale of all property shall at no time have less restrictions than recorded by the Dell Realty Corporation as of July 1, 1941."

Mr. Pol dug deeper. By checking the real estate records in the town of New Milford, he found the Declaration of Restrictions. In it was this statement about Birch Groves:

"Said premises shall not be used or occupied in any manner by any person of Negro, Hebrew, or Jewish descent or extraction."

Pol gathered together the facts and, in July 1957, submitted a written complaint to the Connecticut Commission on Civil Rights:

I believe that the Birch Groves Association is a place of public accommodation within the definition of the laws of Connecticut insofar as it provides water through a community water system to all property owners . . . and maintains the roads within the community. As such, it may not under the laws of Connecticut engage in racial or religious discrimination. It is my belief . . . that I have been denied membership in the Association and threatened with termination of my right of access to the community water system solely because I am of the Jewish faith.

When the Association learned of Pol's complaint to the Commission, it decided not to shut off the water at that time but to bring suit against Pol and another Jew, a lawyer, who also had a place in Birch Groves. The Association's complaint against the lawyer was that he had not paid his water assessments because he felt they were discriminatory. As a nonmember of the Association, the lawyer had been assessed for water at a rate higher than the highest fee paid by Association members for *all* facilities, including road maintenance, use of beach and tennis courts, and the like.

The Association's suits were filed in December 1957. Two and a half years later, in August 1960, in Litchfield County's Court of Common Pleas, Judge Walter J. Sidor made his ruling. He ruled for the Association, declaring that Pol's claim of discrimination was not borne out by the evidence, and that the Association was not required to furnish water. In the case of the lawyer, he ruled that $54 a year was fair for the water he had used. The lawyer paid, and his case was closed.

The Pols—who, on advice of counsel, had also refused to pay the discriminatory water rates—were still not in the clear. In November, they received a letter and a bill from the Association. The letter said:

"If payment is not received by December 15, 1960, you will no longer be served by the Birch Groves water system."

The bill stated that the Pols owed $108.75 for the current year and $372 for the preceding four years. A notation read:

"Interest @ 6% on unpaid balance—$60.49"—in actuality, 16¼ per cent on $372.

Pol sent the Association a check for $270, for five yearly payments of $54, together with a letter explaining that this was the amount Judge Sidor had determined as a fair charge.

The Association sent back a letter, notifying Pol that it was crediting him with this payment, but insisting that the bill as originally submitted was correct and warning that its bill "must still be paid before December 15, 1960, or water service to your home will be shut off. . . ."

"The judge's ruling had made impossible an appeal on the basis of discrimination," Pol said. "The Civil Rights Commission had decided they had no jurisdiction in the case. We felt it would be immoral of us to pay the bill at the discriminatory rate. We wondered what would happen."

On the Sunday before Christmas, 1960, the Pols found out. Their water was shut off. Since then they have managed as best they can by getting their drinking water in gallon jugs from a neighbor and for other purposes using unfit-for-drinking water from an old well they rehabilitated in the basement of their house.

The Association is well aware of the Pols' plight. To date it has made no move to do away with its discriminatory provisions so that the Pols can have community services on the same basis as other residents.

Evidently, once racial and religious prejudice takes hold as it has done in Birch Groves on Candlewood Lake in the town of New Milford, Litchfield County, Connecticut, such things as water rights are considered more important than human rights—at least by those who establish and support discrimination.

Jews have been hardest hit by two devices designed to bar them from entire neighborhoods: club-membership and cooperative- or nonprofit-membership plans.

The club-membership plan applies principally to home ownership. Under this scheme no one may buy into a neighborhood unless he is acceptable to the board of the community club. Theoretically, this is a good example of community self-rule, a kind of decentralized self-government that should be encouraged in a society that tends toward concentration of power in the hands of federal or state government at the expense of the local community. Practically, however, the result in many places has been deliberate exclusion of Jews from home ownership in what amounts to a closed community.

The case of B. J. Harris *versus* the Sunset Island Property Owners, Inc., of Dade County, in the Miami Beach area of Florida, is another classic example of the devious practice of the club membership plan.

Harris, a Jew, purchased a lot on Sunset Island No. 2. Like all other lots in the area, this one was subject to a recorded covenant that barred ownership of any lots on the island to persons not members in good standing of Sunset Island

Property Owners. At the time Harris purchased the land, the bylaws of the property-owners provided that no member of the corporation could sell or lease any property to any person "not of the Caucasian race, or who is not a Gentile, or who has been convicted of a felony . . . , nor can any person who falls into any of these categories become a member of the corporation."

After purchasing the property, Harris received a membership application blank from the corporation. Aware that he was ineligible for membership because he was Jewish, Harris refused to apply. But he proceeded to build a house on the lot and to move into it. The corporation started a lawsuit to compel Harris to vacate his home and to divest himself of ownership of the property, on the ground that he was not a member of the corporation. Before filing this complaint, the corporation amended its bylaws to eliminate the provision banning membership to non-Caucasians, non-Gentiles, and felons. Instead, the corporation substituted an ambiguous bylaw requiring applicants for membership to be "of good moral character." Harris applied for membership under this new bylaw. He was rejected, presumably on the grounds of character.

Eventually, the case was decided for Harris. The Florida Supreme Court ruled that

the original requirement of membership, in the specific exclusion of Jews, constituted an illegal and unenforceable restraint on these appellants (Mr. & Mrs. Harris) at the time they acquired the property.[38]

However, the court cautioned that it was *not* holding invalid all requirements that property-owners be members of a property-owners' association (and that membership be limited to persons of good moral character). Thus, the new-found subterfuge of the Sunset Island Property Association, although applied too late for the Harris case, might apply in the future. This association, and others like it, could prevent Jews from becoming members on the arbitrary grounds of character unfitness—to be determined by themselves alone. Once excluded from the association in question, a Jew could be prevented by law from building and occupying a home in the association's neighborhood—unless he could prove his exclusion was based upon his religion.

The cooperative plan for apartments may be abused in the same way. (The cooperative plan provides for apartments to be purchased from a cooperative corporation with an all-powerful directorate.) In those cases where the directorate is anti-Semitic, the end results are the same as in the club membership plan.

The following is a statistical analysis of how this particular device to circumvent the Supreme Court decision on restrictive covenants actually operates. The information is from the files of the Anti-Defamation League.

One Sunday in 1958 *The New York Times* printed sixty advertisements of apartments for rent or sale in its large real estate section. Interested parties were invited to telephone for further information.

In about 8 per cent of the cases in the ADL inquiry-experiment, the caller with the Jewish-sounding name received a different response and treatment from the caller with the non-Jewish-sounding name. In half of those cases (4 per cent of the calls), the "non-Jewish" applicants were told that the apartments were in buildings that had no Jewish tenants. The difference in treatment between presumed Jewish applicants and presumed non-Jewish applicants was noticeable. Since a number of the apartments were for cooperative sale, the relative absence of Jewish owners from cooperatives becomes explainable on discriminatory grounds.

Club-membership and cooperative-ownership plans are only two of the devices that currently prevent Jews from obtaining access to the housing they seek. A number of other techniques not yet described deserve mention.

The so-called Van Sweringen Covenant makes the sale of a property contingent on the consent of the original owner of the undeveloped tract. This ostensibly forces all future owners of developed tracts—including homes—to sell only to parties of whom the original owner approves—that is to say, only to non-Jews.

"Joint consent for building" requires that the four adjoining owners of land must agree to a sale of a tract for building purposes. This apparently permits a single anti-Semitic property-holder in the neighborhood to prevent a Jew from buying property for the purpose of housing—despite the wishes of any of the other neighbors.

In "joint consent for sales," two (not four) adjoining owners must agree to a sale, or the seller purportedly stands to forfeit five hundred dollars in damages.

Under the "leasehold plan," the occupant leases the land for ninety-nine years and may not sell the building without the consent of the community's overseers. To qualify as a purchaser, he must have lived in the area for a year. This is intended to make both renting and purchase of a home dependent on the community management's pleasure.

Real estate agents who enter into "broker's agreements" individually or through associations undertake not to rent or sell property to certain groups. In many communities, these limitations are incorporated into "codes of ethics." We have already noted how these codes are enforced against reluctant brokers and builders.

Lenders resort to "mortgagees' agreements." Those who sign up will not make mortgage loans where there is the "threat" that an "undesirable" group will move into an area en masse. In these cases, some lenders will not lend money for mortgages even when the government is willing to insure them.

There are many other devices. All have one common purpose: to circumvent the spirit of the Supreme Court decision by making it possible, through self-enforcing agreements, for realtors, builders, property- and home-owners and lenders to prevent Jews from moving into non-Jewish neighborhoods. And all have a common rationale: Jews force down the value of the property in the neighborhood in which they purchase homes. This Gresham's Law of Neighborhoods theory has gained wide currency and deserves careful examination. What are its fallacies? What, if any, are the truths?

To begin with, we must concede that the Gresham's Law of Neighborhoods has a certain foundation in experience. The fear that when a minority group moves into a neighborhood in large numbers the neighborhood will lose its economic value is partly true. But it is not the whole truth. Infiltration of neighborhoods by minorities is not the cause of property depreciation; the true cause is the panicky flight from that neighborhood of the old inhabitants, a classic case of what social psychologists term a "self-fulfilling prophecy" —by which they mean that people, acting hysterically, often produce the very effects they fear. "I feared a fear and it has come to pass. And that of which I was in terror has come upon me," in the words of the book of Job. Abandoning a neighborhood out of fear lest new neighbors turn it into a slum, the old residents set the stage for a slum. The old residents themselves begin the process of the depreciation of property in the neighborhood by hastily selling their homes, often for prices considerably below real value.

What would happen—and what has happened—when residents have not become frightened by the specter of minority neighbors, when they have regarded a new neighbor as an individual to be judged on his own merits, not prejudged as a stereotype of danger? Wherever "new" people have been permitted to move into established neighborhoods on an

individual basis, experience has shown that the neighborhood has continued to prosper, even increase in value.

Why would such new neighbors wish to lower, rather than
enhance, the economic value of their property in a desirable
neighborhood?

This is no simple ABC proposition; real estate values are
notorious for their fluctuation, depending not merely on
time and place but also on how people feel about time and
place. The economics of real property are sometimes con-
fused by epidemics of selling and buying that take place without regard to the objective situation of desirability in terms
of site, utilities, transportation, and so forth.

Several serious books have recently examined the complex-
ities of a situation the nuances of which the Gresham's Law
of Neighborhoods disregards. These books deal with a number of minorities, not merely Jews. In this connection it must
be repeated that, though American Jews are far less handicapped in housing opportunities than other groups, they
still suffer from the same basic disabilities as Negroes, Puerto
Ricans, and other nonwhite groups.

In a carefully controlled analysis of 10,000 housing sales
Luigi M. Laurenti conclusively destroys the myth that the
entry of nonwhites always depresses property values.[39]

In seven detailed case studies of cities in the South and
North, Nathan Glazer and Davis McEntire show the different
factors that do affect minority housing opportunities.[40]

Two of the factors have already been mentioned: the idea
of homogeneity and the idea of status. Applied to neighborhoods, they are used to justify discrimination. How accurate—
or, rather, how realistic—are they?

It is an illusion that status can be fixed in America once
and for all. The most effective demonstration is the experience of the Jewish group itself. Beginning mostly as
impoverished immigrants working mainly as factory laborers
and small peddlers, within one or two generations a large

percentage of their group was able to climb the economic ladder into professional and commercial occupations. This was possible because American life is fluid. Part of the fluidity of American economic society can be attributed to our geographic mobility. American industry is constantly on the move, from one part of the country to another. As it moves, it draws the labor force with it.

In the long run, the ideal of permanent neighborhoods in which residents are able to select their own neighbors by applying preconceptions of desirability is doomed. The job situation determines the flow of population, and with it the flow of various groups in and out of neighborhoods.

These two movements—economic and geographic—join to undermine the notion of self-enclosed neighborhoods. So long as Americans can move up the economic ladder with relative freedom, they have the ability to move up culturally and socially and residentially as well.

Status in America is associated with education and cultural background—but so is economic success, which is becoming more and more impossible without superior education. In turn, education raises those who benefit from it to a higher cultural level, entitling them to higher social status, symbolized by (among other external things) better homes in better neighborhoods.

The question is not whether Jewish professionals and businessmen can meet the social standards of their Christian counterparts; among their economic peers they already *are* social peers. No objective criterion can assign a Jewish physician status lower than that of a non-Jewish physician, a Jewish textile manufacturer lower status than a non-Jewish textile manufacturer. They do the same work, read the same books, play the same games—although perhaps still in different clubs—and furnish their homes with the same quality of furniture.

The dream of homogeneous neighborhood is a fantasy because it shuts out the daylight of reality: American society is not homogeneous. Whatever some people may imagine, there is no *one* dominant central majority as distinct from a number of fringe minorities. It has often been observed that the United States is a nation of minorities; the so-called majority is merely a fluctuating term for various conjunctions of minority aggregates. No more than half of the country's inhabitants are white Protestants of Anglo-Saxon ancestry—and the words *white* and *Protestant* should be in quotation marks. Anthropologists agree that, except in remote parts of the earth, very few human beings belong to a "pure" human stock; and *Protestant* is a term covering many sects.

The supposed majority of Protestants in the United States ranges in religious views from Fundamentalist to Episcopalian. Nor can the term *Christian* be substituted to indicate a unified majority of Americans. Among Catholics, we find diocesan groupings of communities that are predominantly Irish, Polish, Italian, Greek, Puerto Rican, Spanish, and Negro.

Similarly, Jews cannot be regarded as a single-unit minority, either from the religious or the secular point of view. Jews have a strong sense of kinship and of mutual responsibility. Nevertheless, in face of all their feeling for brotherhood, the Jews in the United States have adopted the American principle of voluntary organization. There are large and distinct Orthodox, Conservative, and Reform congregational movements for those Jews whose identification with Judaism is mostly religious. American Jews who prefer to belong to the Jewish group as secularists join other associations—social-welfare, Zionist, education, or purely recreational.

Confusing as it may seem to those who wish to simplify the religious–ethnic groupings in the United States into a direct majority–minority relationship, there is a kind of public recognition in this country that no one religious group may presume to speak for the majority of religionists. On public occasions, the so-called "American Religion" is represented by minister and/or priest and/or rabbi—and, on particularly auspicious occasions, by representatives of all three categories. Thus, the United Service Organizations, insofar as it ministers to the spiritual needs of armed forces personnel, is composed of representative bodies of all faiths; each of these representations, in turn, is carefully representative of the sects that make up the various elements in its church.

In sum, these two factors alone—the mobility of American society and its heterogeneity—make it impossible for any given neighborhood to control its inhabitants over the long run. That is why American neighborhoods so often have completely changed hands, and older residents have moved out when "undesirable elements" have moved in.

Can nothing be done about this? How can the average American be made to understand that to segregate himself in one neighborhood and to segregate "the others" in another neighborhood does not answer his need for status?

Basically, it is a question of self-education in democratic attitudes and human values. It is also a question that deeply involves our nation's educational system.

III. DISCRIMINATION IN HIGHER EDUCATION

●

example

MARJORIE WEBSTER JUNIOR COLLEGE
Rock Creek Park Estates
Washington 12, D.C.
January 16, 1961

Office of Admissions

Dear Applicant:

This college operates on a quota system between faiths, foreign students and geographical distribution. We appreciate your interest in applying for admission but regret to have to advise that our quota of students of the Jewish faith is filled. Accordingly your check for registration and pictures are being returned herewith.

Sincerely yours,

Frieda Hildenbrand
Director of Admissions

ASHLEY HALL SCHOOL FOR GIRLS
Charleston, S.C.

July 29, 1959

Dear Mrs. _____

I am sorry that I must return your application and entrance fee for your daughter's admission here in 1961.

We appreciate your interest in the school but we have found that it is a wise policy not to accept students of religious faiths different from the majority of the girls here.

While we are a non-sectarian school, our resident girls are all members of Christian churches. Past experience has taught us that the Jewish girls find it difficult to fit into our schedules because of different times of church services and religious holidays.

Sincerely,

Carolina Pardue
Headmistress

Education has always been stressed in the United States; one result has been an increasing proportion of college-educated population. According to figures compiled by the National Industrial Conference Board, there has been a remarkable growth in educational attainment in industry during the past twenty years. In 1940, only one worker in eighteen held a college diploma; in 1960, one out of every ten workers was a college graduate. Today more than half the nation's workers have completed high school, compared to one third of the workers of twenty years ago. In the words of Algo D. Henderson, "Education, and especially higher education, has replaced free land and abundant natural resources as the best route to individual success and personal advancement in this country."[41]

Where do the college graduates work? The largest group of college graduates are in the professional occupations—a broad category that covers, among hundreds of others, doctors, lawyers, airplane pilots, musicians, newspapermen, foresters, and funeral directors. A century or even fifty years ago, only doctors and lawyers needed diplomas. Now, increasingly, with the tremendous mechanization of the American economy and the introduction of automation, more trained technical workers are needed.

American Jews have long been in the forefront in the national drive for a college education; as early as 1908, when the Immigration Commission surveyed seventy-seven educational institutions, 8.5 per cent of the male student body was composed of first- and second-generation Jews, although Jews at that time made up only some 2 per cent of the total population. Jewish students were 13 per cent of those studying law, 18 per cent of those preparing for pharmacy.[42] A recent study, based on United States Census information, noted:

Two religious groups stand out above all others as well-educated; those with Jewish and those with Episcopalian religious preferences. A third group, the Presbyterian, had attained an educational level considerably above the average. More than one-fifth of the members of each of these groups were college graduates, and only a comparatively small per cent had less than 8 years of schooling. More than 60 per cent of the household heads in each of these groups were high school graduates, whereas among the general population only 40 per cent had this much schooling. . . .[43]

From 1955 to 1956, American household heads who had four years or more of college education were: Episcopal, 22.6 per cent; Jewish, 22.3 per cent; Presbyterian, 13 per cent.

The B'nai B'rith Vocational Service Bureau reported in 1957 that American Jewish young people were as interested as their parents in college education:

While an estimated 62 out of every 100 college-age Jewish persons are actually enrolled in college, only about 27 out of every

100 non-Jews are in college. . . . Our figures indicate that the proportion of college students in the Jewish population is about 2⅔ times as great as the proportion of college students in the general population (4 per cent as compared with 1.6 per cent).[44]

One observer of a well-to-do Massachusetts suburb noted: "Well over 80 per cent of the Jewish children who graduated from Newton High School in 1958 . . . are attending colleges and universities. This pattern is generally characteristic of Jewish suburbia throughout the nation."[45]

While Jewish boys and girls have always been a minority in any national high school classification—some 5 per cent of the senior class and 10 per cent of the college applicants—nearly half of the Jewish students made a try at getting to college, against 14 per cent of the corresponding Protestants and 11 per cent of the Catholics, although the Protestant and Catholic students had a greater possibility than the Jews of admission to the college of their choice.

The admissions hurdle over which some Jewish students trip—thereby reducing their fair proportion of acceptances—is called the "quota system." There can be no simple definition of the practice. It takes many shapes from campus to campus, changing in form although not in purpose. The quota system is an understanding (sometimes a rule) which says (sometimes orally, sometimes cryptically formulated in writing) that it is best for the educational institution in question to permit no more than a given percentage of Jews to matriculate as students (the figure can range from a fraction of a per cent all the way up to a substantial amount). As quickly as the arbitrarily agreed-upon percentage of Jews is completed in any given year, the remaining Jewish applicants are, so to speak, out of the running. In short, the quota has been filled.

At the very outset of this discussion, the position of the Anti-Defamation League should be made eminently clear:

The admissions barriers that today confront Jewish applicants on American college campuses are not nearly as high as they once were, but they are still clearly present.

It is not uncommon for Jews to point an accusing finger at the unjust quota system as an effective tactic for limiting Jewish enrollment. However, any serious description of anti-Semitism in the United States as it applies to higher education must also examine a number of other, interrelated factors. These have been excellently summarized in the staff reports of the New York State Commission that studied the need for a state university:

Youth sometimes encounter difficulties in gaining admission to college because of their race, creed, color, or national origin. These factors, as well as economic and geographic barriers, have no relationship to the ability of youth; nevertheless, they constitute barriers to attendance. An individual may be affected by one or more of the factors: wealth, place of residence, academic qualification, race, creed, color, or national origin. *Because the various barriers are interrelated, however, a cause-and-effect relationship between college attendance and one type of barrier separate from the others cannot be shown. The fact that this interrelationship between the several types of barriers exists should be kept in mind.* [Italics ours.][46]

Let us review the various factors mentioned—the socio-economic, geographic, and purely academic, as well as the factor of anti-Semitic discrimination, to see how Jewish students were affected by the conjunction of the various factors.

How are American Jewish students who wish to attend college affected by the socio-economic position of their families and group?

The cost of an undergraduate university or college education in 1960 has been estimated at from $7500 to $10,000 for students at private institutions. A professional education is far more costly. Dr. Howard Rusk analyzes the expenses of medical training, for example, as follows:

Currently, the estimated cost of training a general practitioner is $47,000, a specialist $67,000. These costs include tuition and books for four years of college and four years of medical school, plus the loss of potential earnings during the period of education, the year of interneship, and during the average of three years of residency training for the specialists. Living expenses are not included.[47]

College students are usually in no position to pay their own way. They must depend on parents and/or scholarships. While it is true that the number and value of scholarships have risen markedly since the end of World War II, they are still insufficient to meet the constantly growing cost of a college education. Still, the fact remains that most of the applicants for scholarships come from families with an average income of over $8000, who are willing and able to supplement scholarships.

Since the average annual income of Americans is $4000-plus, would-be college students whose families have average or even slightly above-average income face a severe financial problem, even with scholarship aid. This influences applications; students from these families are less likely to apply for college. In 1949, the American Council on Education reported on the findings of a sample study:

The highest rates of both academic achievement and application to college occurred among the children of professional men, executives, small-business proprietors, and white-collar workers.

Large numbers of American Jews work in these occupations. Thus the relatively large number of American Jewish young people applying to colleges and universities are reflecting a national rather than a strictly Jewish pattern.

Some people mistakenly believe that American Jews have

an edge over non-Jews in their economic background—a popular misconception. American Jews do not dominate the professions and business, proportionately or numerically. Among religious groups, the Episcopalians (and probably the Unitarians, as well) have larger proportions in professional and technical occupations. The Presbyterians are concentrated in these occupations only slightly less than the Jews.[48]
Reviewing the socio-economic factor as it affects American Jewish young people who apply for admission to institutions of higher learning, we have a plus and minus that cancel each other. American Jewish students benefit from the educational background and economic status of their families, but no more so than with the sons and daughters of other groups in the population with similar or better background qualifications. The Jewish students must, of course, compete with such applicants for admission to the schools of their choice.

Choice of college is definitely related to the geographic factor. In the American Council on Education study cited above, more than half of all students living in urban areas who applied for college admission lived in the Northeast—the area in which American Jews are highly concentrated. Thus, Jewish students living in the Northeast are competing locally with the heaviest concentration of applicants. They are also competing for the most desirable colleges and universities, since Northeastern institutions, on the whole, have the highest national ratings and prestige. Competition for admission to these schools is most intense, for Northeastern students also have to contend with aspirants from all over the country. With so many applicants and with standards that are set so high, it is natural that only the best-qualified students can hope to secure entrance.

This newspaper report (May 1960) describes admissions to Ivy League colleges:

The eight colleges known as Ivy League are Columbia, Harvard, Yale, Princeton, Dartmouth, Brown, the University of Pennsylvania, and Cornell. Together these colleges accepted 13,630 students to fill a total of 8,545 places for their September freshman classes. The same Ivy League mailing included 25,470 rejections. More high school seniors, 1,200 to 1,300, remain on waiting lists.

The reason for the "over-admission" of 5,085 students is that none of the colleges knows how many of the accepted students will accept them; many have applied to more than one Ivy League institution.

Considering that this fall's total freshmen class in all the nation's colleges and universities will be about 900,000 students, the total number of 8,545 Ivy League freshmen may seem to signify much ado about nothing. But in the age that seeks status, the heat generated by the pressure over "getting in" to these prestige colleges is considerable. It should be added that this pressure is still largely confined to the Eastern part of the nation.

Despite attempts at scientific criteria in admissions, the experts concede that the final judgment may be both unfair and unavoidably haphazard in many instances. Harvard rejections include a "statement" that reads:

"We are well aware of the difficulty of making reliable evaluations of intangible personal qualities in examining the records of so many hundreds of students. The evidence is frequently so inadequate or conflicting, and the committee operates under great pressure. . . . Another committee might well have made different decisions in a good many cases."[49]

In view of these problems, American Jewish applicants who favor schools for their nearness to home *and* for their high standards face large odds against being accepted. In addition, there is "internal competition"—the competition among Jewish students themselves. Primarily because of cultural considerations (the long-standing Jewish emphasis on the value of education is one of them), even Jewish families that, objectively speaking, cannot *afford* to send children to college make every sacrifice to do so. Hence, with the general American drive for education reinforced by the Jewish cultural encouragement at home, proportionately more Jewish students than students from other groups apply for admission to college. Facing a quota system, the odds thus become even higher against the admission of a Jewish student to the school of his first choice.

Evidence is available to prove that discrimination against Jewish applicants when it appears is directed against *certain Jewish students living in the Northeast and in large cities.*[50] The chief victims of this discrimination are upper-class Jewish students who rank in the upper fifth of their class scholastically, who are distinguished by their activity in student affairs, who are at least third-generation American, and whose fathers had gone to college before them.

Jewish students with such splendid records naturally crowd the doors of the "best" schools in the Northeast with contradictory results. The paradox is that the more Jewish students resembled the type most acceptable to college admissions offices, the more they were turned away by institutions of their first choice.

Finally, there is the factor of active discrimination. Certainly, the other factors—wealth, place of residence, academic qualifications—play a part in the rejection of Jewish applicants for admission to college. They are competing with many students whose parents are equally well-to-do, who live in the same part of the country, who are equally well qualified academically. Insofar as this is true, if Jewish applicants simply suffer from the same difficulties in gaining admission as other students, no one would have a right to charge that they are the victims of educational discrimination.

Unfortunately, a number of studies over the years have shown that the average Jewish college or university appli-

cant in the United States has a considerably smaller chance
of acceptance than an applicant who is Catholic or Protestant.
In the Northeast, where 80 per cent of the Jewish applications are made, the bright Jewish student is at a clear disadvantage in comparison to an equally bright Catholic or
Protestant student.

For example, compare the fate of Jewish with non-Jewish
applications in New York state.

For every hundred applications by non-Jewish students,
there are thirty-three applications by Jews to the fourteen
nonsectarian liberal arts colleges in the state. But one hundred non-Jews are accepted for every twenty-six Jews. In
graduate schools, the discrepancy becomes more glaring.
Jewish students who graduate in the top fourth of their college class have more difficulty than non-Jews, regardless of
the non-Jew's academic rating, in gaining admission to institutions offering advanced professional training.[51]

What of the less favored schools, outside New York state
and the Northeast? Cannot American Jews be content to
accept second-best? Unfortunately, the same pattern exists
throughout the country: relatively high acceptance rates for
applications received from Protestant and Catholic applicants, relatively low acceptance rates for applications received
from Jewish youth. State universities favor residents of the
state, and many private schools impose quotas restricting the
proportion of Jewish students.

Still, Jewish youth *do* secure admission to colleges, to
some extent a tribute to the remarkable persistence of the
Jewish applicants. Anxious to attend college and all too
aware of the chance that they will be refused at the college
of their first choice, Jewish students tend to apply to many
colleges at the same time. They make three or four times as
many applications as Protestants and Catholics. Reasonably
enough, they argue that they are bound to be accepted by one

of the colleges—if not by their first or second choice, perhaps by their third or fourth.

"All's well that ends well." What does "a little discrimination" matter so long as he can eventually achieve a college education? What does it matter if it is not the school he has set his heart on?

The Jewish students who apply in increasing numbers for a decreasing number of college-entrance opportunities every year cannot wait. In fact, now is the strategic time to alter the discriminatory pattern where it exists. During the next ten years, the number of high school seniors who are potential college material is expected to double. If Jewish young people are at a minor disadvantage in securing admission to college in the early 1960s, they will be at a major disadvantage when the ranks of applicants swell, particularly since the number of classes, classrooms, and teachers cannot keep up with the number of students. If Jewish youth are often forced to compromise for a second- or third-choice education now, what may they look forward to in 1970 or 1975? If ever the college quota system is going to be remedied, for purely practical reasons this is the time to do so.

The colleges themselves are aware that delay is dangerous. As long ago as 1954, the American Council on Education found that since "college admission practices will become more selective and possibly more discriminatory," colleges must be encouraged "to formulate policies which will lead, during the coming time of high enrollment pressure, to college admission procedures based primarily on the ability of applicants."

It is bad for American society as a whole that any group of Americans, alert and energetic though it may be, cannot realize its full potentialities. For example, today there is a great need for physicians, yet prospective physicians are being kept out of some medical schools because they are Jewish.

The same has been true in the recent past of would-be engineers, accountants, and lawyers.

Studies of manpower utilization, such as those conducted during the past decade by Eli Ginzberg, show the vast loss to the national economy resulting from the failure of our universities to train large numbers of professionals and technicians.[52] Part of the reason for this failure is the refusal to lower prejudicial barriers against minority groups. Enlightened self-interest alone dictates the lowering of those barriers, if the United States is to realize its economic potential.

The argument for restricting Jewish university applicants is certainly not defensible on social grounds. To demand that one group of Americans should learn to accept second best in education, second-class citizenship, and second-class social status as a fact of American life is to accept America at its lowest standards. Manifestly, the principle of superior and inferior rights is contrary to American democracy and undermines the unity of American society. The Jew who is rejected by the school of his choice for reasons that have nothing to do with his innate ability or demonstrated achievement questions both the intrinsic worth and the values of a society that countenances such admission practices. He reasons that if he must adjust to this fact of American life, then he must also "adjust" to inequality, favoritism, snobbishness, and outright chicanery. The society he is being introduced to, if its universities are its high exemplars, is stratified, exclusionist, hypocritical. And when he eventually does secure admission to his second- or third-choice university, he must learn to live in a situation in which these undesirable undemocratic but *real* values are practical.

Who is to blame for this unhappy state of affairs? Although the university is part of a complex society, in the end it is the total community life that educates. This does not mean that the burden of responsibility for discriminatory admissions practices by the offending colleges and universities can be shifted to a vague scapegoat called "the community." Even though in practicing discrimination it is true that some universities are adopting a general American social practice, they should be conscious of the part of their role that calls for actively setting standards rather than merely being passive practitioners of a limited kind of "practice for living." The true attitudes of the policy formulators and those who carry out these policies are hard to assess; that they are both mixed and revocable is apparent from this informed comment:

Of the present unhappy fact of discrimination in college admissions we have abundant evidence. But as yet we do not have anything like the same amount or kind of evidence as to the attitudes that prompt such discriminating methods of selection. The evidence we do have tends to indicate that the institutions involved are much less aware of any intention to discriminate than the results of their methods would suggest. One explanation is obvious, of course,—it is concealed discrimination, which the discriminators have the grace to be ashamed of even if they do not have the candor to acknowledge it. But it is probable that a good deal of discrimination is due to the incidental and not always fully considered implications and consequences of admission policies.[53]

The quota system is the prime example of an admissions policy whose discriminatory implications and consequences are concealed, unacknowledged, or rationalized. Under the quota system, students from all parts of the country, from different religious and racial groups, and from varying economic and social backgrounds are enrolled at the university according to certain fixed proportions. Asked for an explanation of the quota system, university administrators speak of an ideal social desideratum. They assert that each student body should be representative of the nation as a whole. Specifically, it should not be overburdened with students from the most populous Northeastern region, although

Northeastern high school seniors have the highest academic average and even though the quota system schools are located in the Northeast. Nor should there be an "overrepresentation" of Jewish students, since Jews make up only slightly more than 3 per cent of the total population of the United States. The administrators of these preferred universities admit that education is ideally the universal right of all Americans, but that factually there are just so many school seats, laboratory tables, and dormitory rooms available. In short, the advocates of the quota system practice and preach a *numerus clausus* for Jewish students.

In at least one context, the quota system appeals to larger "national considerations." The President's Commission on Higher Education, the argument begins, has specified the national goal of higher education.[54] This goal says that about half of all youth should have a chance for at least two years of college work after they have completed high school. At the present time, only one third of the seventeen-year-olds in the upper quarter of their classes, and less than one fifth of the second quarter go on to college. Therefore, it is the duty of universities to make room for these deserving prospective students. This reasoning leads to the conclusion that other students have to be sacrificed. The Jews thus become innocent victims, not out of religious or social discrimination, but because they are already enrolled in larger proportions than statistical balance will justify.

Unfortunately, this argument in support of the quota system cannot be taken at face value. If there is any group in the country that is *under*represented in institutions for higher education it is the nonwhite group, particularly the Negroes. Yet the quota system, ostensibly intended to offer opportunities for education to the underprivileged, restricts nonwhites, too.

The Fair Educational Practices legislation that some states have passed serves more to protect prospective Negro students than Jewish applicants. Significantly, some of these laws make it unlawful for schools to ask prospective students to give their race or religious affiliation on their applications for admission. However, in order to weed out undesirables, schools frequently use the device of requesting a photograph of the applicant, which usually establishes race. Other potentially discriminatory questions (the applicant's birthplace, that of his parents, his mother's maiden name, his nationality) can be evaded by misleading or false replies. But a photograph is the clearest clue to a person's race.

Thus the quota system cannot be defended as leading to a more representative student body; Negroes are deliberately underrepresented.

But let us not assume that all colleges are insincere in their protestations that they support a quota system because it insures a representative sampling of Americans of all races and religions. Those who are sincere are mistaken in the means they have adopted to achieve that representation. For there is no objective proof that the members of one group are more than slightly superior intellectually to any other. It is a widespread assumption that the Jewish group is more intelligent than the Negro. Yet:

We note an almost universal principle in respect to overlapping group differences: *the differences within the same group are greater (i.e., the range is wider) than the differences between the averages of the two groups.* For example, we notice that there are many Jewish children who stand lower than the average Negro child, and some Negro children who stand higher than the average Jewish child. We cannot then possibly conclude that all Jews are bright and all Negroes dull. It is even wrong to say the Jews "as a group" are bright, and Negroes "as a group" are dull.[55]

Regarding applicants for college, we are dealing not with the average but with the upper fourth or upper fifth of each group. If colleges were to abolish their quota systems, they would nevertheless acquire the same representative selection of young Americans of all races and religions which they are ostensibly seeking—that is, if students were freely selected on the basis of character and scholastic achievement alone.

The quota system in practice achieves the opposite result. By erecting barriers to the average Jewish student, discriminatory schools admit a disproportionate number of very superior Jewish students relative to the non-Jewish average students who are admitted more liberally. Like all closed systems, the quota system tends to perpetuate itself—in this case, by reinforcing prejudicial attitudes. The system engenders resentment on the part of the average non-Jewish student against the more gifted Jewish student who surpasses him in achievement. This resentment is extended to the Jewish group as a whole and leads to further exclusionary practices.

●

Discrimination and *selection* are the words some Greek-letter fraternities have for it. Every once in a while a scandal breaks that makes men of good will wonder if *fraternity* is perhaps a misnomer for these college societies.

One such scandal broke on February 8, 1961, when the Chicago *Daily News* ran a two-column-headline story in which the lead stated: "A Jewish student at Lake Forest College has been depledged from Phi Delta Theta fraternity because of his religion."

When the boy involved, Donald C. Schiller, was asked to comment on the fraternity's action, he said, in a show of good fellowship: "These are my friends, and I don't want to say anything about it."

In marked contrast to Schiller's statement, subsequent news stories quoted John Shetman, one of the governing members of the national council of Phi Delta Theta, with all indications that he was not only speaking for himself but for the national president and treasurer, as saying:

"The Phi Delta Theta fraternity was founded on Christian

principles and we feel that Christian beliefs must be practiced by the members."

At Lake Forest itself, the administration was deeply concerned. A meeting called by the College's president, William Graham Cole, was attended by a committee of students, faculty, trustees, and alumni. The statement issued after the meeting contained the following:

The long-range committee at Lake Forest College studying the general question of fraternities and sororities, has added to its concern the case of a student depledged by Phi Delta Theta because of his religion (Jewish). The local chapter, interested in the student, pledged him in the hope that the matter would be approved by the national council of Phi Delta Theta, but this was not allowed.

President Cole commended the initial interest of the chapter and expressed the hope that the day will come soon when a group of students will take additional steps to permit them to choose their own members on a campus. The President cited the resolution of the college's board of trustees [made in May 1958], condemning racial and religious discrimination, but indicated that any action at this time without full review by the study committee would be premature and inappropriate.

Lake Forest College, Dean of Students Howard Hoogesteger admitted, had had problems of discrimination before —as, indeed, have many colleges throughout the United States. In fact, acting president John R. Howard had warned Lake Forest students at a 1959 vesper service in the College chapel that "restrictive covenants . . . reflect the 'pure race' ideology of Nazi Germany. . . . They are antisocial . . . un-Christian . . . immoral. . . . Can a fraternity or sorority refuse to admit a student because of his color or his race or his religion—in direct conflict with the Christian principles that are crucial in the college?"

As reported by the *Daily News* after the Schiller scandal broke, Dean Hoogesteger said that "all Greek letter societies have been urged by the faculty and board of trustees to re-move racially restrictive clauses. Phi Delta Theta does not have one, but 'the national organizations can circumvent this by forcing locals to gain approval of each pledge by the national.' "

Perhaps the strongest stand against discrimination was the May 1958 resolution of the Board of Trustees of Lake Forest College; it was adopted nearly three years before the Schiller case developed. In the opinion of many observers, the statement is a model of enlightenment and forthrightness on the issue of discrimination in college fraternities and sororities. It reads:

As a Christian institution, Lake Forest College opens its doors and facilities to any student on the basis of his or her character and ability to carry satisfactory college work, irrespective of race, religion, or nationality. Therefore, the College expects and requires that all social organizations within the College adhere to the spirit as well as the letter of this principle. Over a period of time fraternities and sororities have become a valued part of the College. Originally the standards on race, religion, and nationality of some of these organizations were not in accord with the stand taken by the College. It is encouraging to see that a large percentage of them are now moving in the direction of policies consistent with the policy of the College. It is hoped that all will do so with the greatest possible speed.

The College recognizes that the full accomplishment of this objective will take time. However, the College must have assurance from all fraternities and sororities and other social organizations which have not achieved this goal that they are moving in the right direction. If it develops that any of these associations refuse to accept the principle of non-discrimination, or after a reasonable time show no progress in this direction, the Board of Trustees has no alternative but to insist upon the removal of such organization from the campus. The local and national chapters of all organizations which do not comply with the stated

principle of the College will be notified of this statement of the
Board of Trustees.

Each fraternity and sorority not now complying with the stated
purpose of the College as to discrimination will be required to
make an annual report to the College documenting direct and
formal efforts in the direction of eliminating discrimination, including the raising of the question with their national officers and
at national conclaves. Faculty advisers to sororities and fraternities are requested to make an independent report on the progress
of the respective groups for which they serve as advisers. A
special committee of the Board of Trustees will annually review
these reports, confer with faculty representatives, officers of the
fraternities and sororities, and recommend appropriate action to
the Board of Trustees.

The Schiller case at Lake Forest aroused national attention, coming as it did on the heels of other similar cases at
other colleges and universities, notably Wisconsin and Stan-
ford.

Throughout February and part of March, the issue of the
right of a college local chapter to pledge a student but to
have him depledged by the national body was a subject not
only for newspaper articles but of intimate concern to Lake
Forest College, as it was to other schools.

Schiller continued to live at the Phi Delta Theta house
while the controversy raged. The local chapter was determined to stick by its pledge and its rights. It was strengthened
in its determination by a Lake Forest College faculty resolution, passed on February 21, which urged college officials
to recognize only those fraternities and sororities which have
such local autonomy and defined this as freedom from restrictions based on race, color, religion, or national origin.
It was further strengthened in its determination by the College president's statement that "Lake Forest College is in
full accord with the local Phi Delta Theta chapter in taking
action to assert their right to choose their own members."

On March 14, at the local chapter's meeting the issue came

to a head; after many hours of discussion and "as a result of our personal feelings as a group of young Americans," as the chapter phrased it, Schiller was repledged in defiance of the national council of Phi Delta Theta, which has 121 chapters and 65,000 members.

The college youngsters further declared that they did "not wish to abandon the national fraternity but hope to improve it," and that they are prepared to go to court to prevent the national fraternity from rescinding their chapter, should the national body do so because of the Schiller issue.

Unfortunately, in April 1961, for reasons that apparently did not relate to the Jewish issue, young Schiller was depledged by the Lake Forest chapter itself. However, in order to keep alive the issue of principle, the local group picked a number of other Jewish pledgees from the student body. At this writing, Phi Delta Theta and four other fraternities on the campus are operating on a basis of local autonomy. In short, at Lake Forest College, the Greek-letter fraternities seem to be determined to have a word for it.

The word is *brotherhood*.

The Jewish college student soon discovers that discrimination does not halt with preferential treatment in admission practices. There are two chief categories of discrimination against Jews in higher education: the first is in admission, the second is in treatment after admission.

A student publication, *Toward a Democratic Campus*, lists areas where students may be treated preferentially:

1. Scholarships, grants, and loans
2. Classroom procedures and curricula
3. Student teacher training
4. College employment practices
5. Student placement
6. Student social organizations
7. Campus housing and boarding
8. Health facilities
9. Physical education
10. Recreation[56]

These areas affect future employment opportunities, equal access in housing and public accommodations, and personal associations. In sum, the entire gamut of discrimination that exists in society as a whole is reproduced in university society. The university is America writ small. A Jewish student is sometimes limited to living in certain neighborhoods, associating only with other Jews, being considered or recommended only for certain jobs. The former president of a small Northeastern college has vividly described housing and social discrimination in the American college:

I have seen the college communities of America divided into exclusive groups which imitate the worst features of a stratified society; with wealthy white gentiles living only with each other while across the road on a less exclusive street live Jewish students in an equally segregated fraternity; in another part of town in boarding homes across the tracks live the "independents," that is, the *déclassés,* where, on tolerance, a few Negro students are allowed to live as well. I have seen dormitories where Jewish students have been segregated by floors on the "educational" grounds that they feel better with their own kind. . . . I know of gentile sorority rules forbidding members to drink Coca-Cola or dance with Jewish fraternity men.[57]

The analogy with the restricted society outside the college campus is striking; here in the institutions of higher learning the discriminatory patterns of the future are being set. Students are being "educated" to discriminate against their "social inferiors."

The "social inferiors" learn quickly how to adjust to this "inferiority." Anticipating the probability of discrimination in housing and friendship opportunities, Jewish university students act like their elders at home. Their parents live and work in or near the larger metropolitan areas. Similarly, Jewish students prefer larger universities where there are a number of other Jewish students with whom they can lead an active, if self-centered, social life without running the risk of deliberate snubs by their non-Jewish schoolmates. The result is deliberate self-segregation, which in turn tends to give basis to the charge of Jewish cliquishness.

Fortunately, there has been important support to the democratization of campus life during the past fifteen years. At the end of World War II, the arrival at universities of a more mature student body, including many veterans, was accompanied by serious concern with the implications of discrimination in higher education. Both students and faculty members became increasingly critical of long-accepted but inequitable institutions, particularly of fraternities and sororities that set up racial and religious barriers to membership. The results of this active criticism have been encouraging:

A few decades ago, a large majority of the 61 national groups included in the National Interfraternity Conference carried restrictive clauses in their constitutions. In 1948, 25 of the total still retained such discriminatory provisions. By 1955 this number had dropped to a total of 10 social fraternities.[58]

(Since 1955 the number of fraternities burdened with restrictive clauses have been reduced from ten to two—and these remaining holdouts have provided "waivers" to local chapters that must comply with antibias campus regulations. The current movement against fraternity discrimination has achieved this relative success because it began within the universities themselves, as part of the self-education of students and faculty alike. What is especially important is that there has been a change of attitude, the growing acceptance of a new concept. William S. Carlson, former president of the State University of New York, has explained the reasons for the educators' concern. Academic and extracurricular programs, he declared, are inseparable. Each is an integral part of the students' education, and "they cannot be severed and each judged by contradictory standards."[59]

In the university, *where* a student lives, and the other students *with whom* he associates are crucial to both the depth and extent of his education; outside the university, where a family lives and those with whom it is friendly are similarly crucial for the depth and extent of its life experience. Restrictions on groups of Americans regarding whom they may associate with and where they may live are in effect restrictions on where they may work, with whom, and at what jobs.

That the recognition of this truth, once clearly presented, is hard to deny is evident from the following statement by the National Interfraternity Conference. The NIC declared that the fraternity is

responsible for a positive contribution to the primary function of colleges and universities, and therefore under an obligation to encourage the most complete personal development of its members, intellectual, physical and social.[60]

Unfortunately, however, the NIC has denied the conclusion that grows out of that statement: that fraternity discrimination retards the educational process by impairing the intellectual growth of students who are accepted for membership as well as those who are rejected.

Nor is the NIC reluctant to lend its platform even to shockingly reactionary views on the subject. In an address delivered on December 1, 1961 in Boston at a meeting of the NIC, one of its speakers argued that fraternities are private associations of men seeking out other men who are congenial. They must, he added, resist those who, no matter their motives, would reshape fraternal life. The speaker was the Rev. James A. McInerney, Professor of Philosophy and Theology at DePaul University in Chicago. He said:

The open, the underhand, the half-hearted attacks on lawfully constituted fraternities and sororities are the result of ignorance or malice. For an institution of higher learning to be guilty of either is unthinkable. To proclaim the attack in the sacred name of patriotism, civil rights, man's humanity or his religion reveals the grossest kind of ignorance.

To belong to a fraternity or not to belong, to prefer this one to that, have nothing to do with a man's patriotism, his duty to mankind or to accurately defined civil rights.

According to the New York *Times,* reporting the story the next day, a sampling of delegate opinion revealed general agreement with Father McInerney; included in the poll were three former national NIC convention chairmen and other such leaders.

The NIC has urged all its member fraternities to join in the fight against the effort by college authorities to force the removal of discriminatory clauses from the bylaws of college fraternities affiliated with national bodies. It is to be regretted that the NIC has taken the position that no college administration has a right to interfere with the autonomy of chapters of national fraternities and that any such interference is an infringement of "the democratic process of self-government" and of "the fundamental principle of free association."

The highest American court, however, has refused to disturb a contrary ruling by a lower federal court. In effect it judicially sanctioned the right of a public-education institution to control policies affecting fraternity organization on its campus.[61] The lower court had held that the State University of New York was justified in ordering the elimination of racial and religious discrimination by fraternities on its twenty-seven campuses. It had decreed that those chapters of national fraternities which have resisted the State University's order were acting contrary to the public interest.[62]

Under the pressure of this ruling and in view of the wide public opinion it represented, (many national fraternities have altered their restrictive charters.) However, many of them still continue to discriminate through "gentlemen's agreements," ritual practices, and other subterfuges.)

So long as the NIC can point to social patterns outside the campus for support of its own discriminatory practices, we may expect opposition to persist against equality of treatment for all students. This is particularly unfortunate, since the campus is in a sense a laboratory from which democratic attitudes and practices, once learned, are carried over to later life.

The old fraternity system met its first important challenge in 1946 at Amherst College, when President Charles W. Cole announced that fraternities on the campus had to abolish racial and religious restrictions within five years. An Amherst College committee comprised mostly of fraternity men summarized in a noteworthy passage the evil of restricted fraternities:

The sense of exclusiveness and social preferment is harmful to the young men who are in the fraternities because it gives them a false and undemocratic sense of superiority and it hurts the students who are outside the fraternities by giving them a wholly unwarranted sense of being inferior and of being social outcasts.[63]

●

Beginning in the late 1940s there was talk of discrimination against Jewish students in the Dental School of Emory University, in Atlanta, Georgia. All through the 1950s, the rumors grew more persistent. Several dentists in Atlanta who were disturbed by the reports made attempts—in 1955, 1956, and in early 1960—to nail them down. Were they true or not? The University officials were noncommittal; there was no concrete evidence at the time and they seemed to feel, in Shakespeare's words, that "Rumour is a pipe/Blown by surmises, jealousies, conjectures. . . ."

The nature of the rumored discrimination was unusual. Since the late 1940s, an abnormally high percentage of Jewish dental students had been flunked out or had been made to repeat courses.

Into the offices of the Anti-Defamation League in Atlanta had come a steady stream of complaints about this situation from Jewish students. To these despairing men, discrimination was a fact, not rumor. Their careers and future were at stake.

Piecing story to story, it became apparent that a turning point in abnormally high flunk-outs and repeats for Jewish students in Emory Dental School had begun in 1948. This was the year that a new Dental School dean was appointed— a Dr. John Buhler.

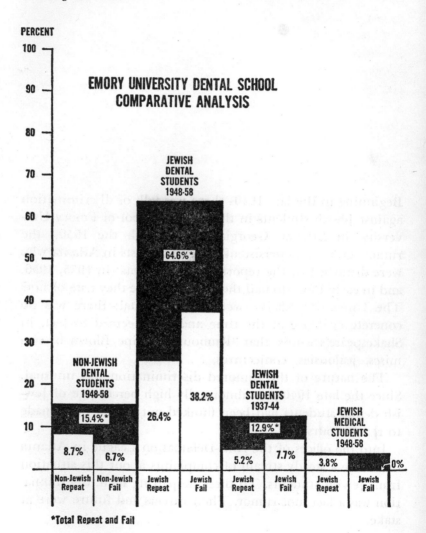

PERCENT

EMORY UNIVERSITY DENTAL SCHOOL
COMPARATIVE ANALYSIS

JEWISH DENTAL STUDENTS 1948-58

64.6%*

NON-JEWISH DENTAL STUDENTS 1948-58

15.4%*

JEWISH DENTAL STUDENTS 1937-44

38.2%

12.9%*

JEWISH MEDICAL STUDENTS 1948-58

8.7%   6.7%   26.4%   5.2%   7.7%   3.8%   0%

Non-Jewish Repeat | Non-Jewish Fail | Jewish Repeat | Jewish Fail | Jewish Repeat | Jewish Fail | Jewish Repeat | Jewish Fail

*Total Repeat and Fail

By 1960, the complaints were so persistent that the Atlanta office of ADL undertook to gather the facts. In due course, it came up with them. They were startling:

1. In 1948–58, 64 per cent of the Jewish students had to repeat or were flunked out, while only 15 per cent of the Christian students had such experiences.

2. In comparison, figures for 1937 through 1944 (which would include students graduating before the 1948 appointment of Dean Buhler) revealed that only 13 per cent of the Jewish students had experienced such inordinate difficulties. A further comparison was made with the 1948–58 Jewish students in Emory University's Medical School, which revealed only a 3.8 per cent repeat rate and no failures.

3. During the 1948–58 period, Christian students admitted came from twenty-eight states, Puerto Rico, and the British West Indies. The Jewish students came from either Georgia or from two other Southern states which, as members of the Southern Regional Compact, paid the Dental School a large subvention ($1500 per student) in addition to the students' tuition fees. Among the states from which Christian students came but Jewish students did not were New York, New Jersey, and Connecticut, all of which usually furnish large numbers of candidates for dental schools. During the 1937–44 period, Jewish students had been admitted from ten states, including these three.

In the middle of December 1960, a group of Atlanta Jewish Community leaders presented the ADL facts and figures to Dr. Walter Martin, president of the University, and Mr. Boisfeuillet Jones, vice-president in charge of Medical Services, which include both the Medical and Dental Schools.

The University administration promised to investigate. On January 5, 1961, Dr. Martin sent a letter to the head of the ADL committee that the matter was still under investigation, but that action was being delayed by the fact that Boisfeuillet

Jones was leaving for a post in Washington, D.C. However, Dr. Martin assured the committee that he would work closely with Dean Buhler and would get in touch with the committee "when we have something definite to report."

Weeks passed; no report.

Early in March, two significant events occurred. On March 8 the ADL was apprised of the fact that Emory University had issued a new application blank for admission to its Dental School, which differed from the University's other application forms in a most curious fashion. It was keyed to various coded classifications, among which was religion and race, separately designated. Under *race*, the code was divided into Caucasian, Jew, and Other.

The following day there was another development. A two-page mimeographed questionnaire was distributed by dental-faculty members to all the students in the Dental School, requesting details of personal knowledge of discrimination based on the religion or the race of the student. The dental students were shocked; the Jewish students among them were both shocked and worried. Although students were not required to affix a signature to the questionnaire, they were requested to fill it out in their own handwriting.

As one student put it at the time: "Having written thousands of words since coming to Emory Dental, it wouldn't take a Sherlock Holmes to match handwriting and student!"

Both the application and the questionnaire were immediately called to the attention of the University administration by the committee. The administration promised to throw out the offensive forms and take prompt action on the entire question of discrimination in the Dental School.

A meeting was held several weeks later, on April 3, at which not only members of the committee and the University administration, including Dean Buhler, were present, but also several members of the Dental School faculty, two rabbis, and two members of the Emory Board of Visitors. The meeting, which Dr. Martin said he hoped would "clear the air," was replete with charges and counter-charges and ended inconclusively. The air remained far from clear.

A few days later it cleared considerably. On April 11 Dean Buhler announced his resignation from the dental faculty, effective at the end of the June quarter, to become vice-president of a dental-instrument manufacturing company.

Two weeks later, on April 25, Dr. Martin sent a letter to a leading member of the committee:

"You brought to our attention a matter that involved principles which are important to all of us," Dr. Martin wrote in part. "I am sure that our discussions have served to remind all of us that, despite our constant vigilance, there is always the possibility that someone may err, even without conscious or deliberate intent. I believe, therefore, that our discussions have brought about an immediate constructive result. We are hopeful that every member of your group has been reassured of the firm policy of this University to treat all students alike . . . to follow this policy consistently in all areas of the University's activities. We earnestly hope that such embarrassing lapses as the grossly misworded application blank will not recur. We are sincerely sorry for the resentment this sheet has caused. We are confident that considerable and lasting good will come from this experience, painful as it may have been to all of us involved, and hope that from it we may have achieved some closer relationship and understanding with the Jewish community in general as well as with the members of your committee."

Here the matter rests. But all concerned—students, faculty, administration, community—are convinced that the long period of foul air at Emory University Dental School caused by religious discrimination has been finally cleared—for good.

The social and housing discrimination practiced against some undergraduates in American universities is reprehensible. In the case of the graduate or professional schools, the same discrimination frequently assumes a more serious character. On the more advanced level, it is not merely a question of Jews being forced to content themselves with slightly inferior universities, fraternities, and dormitories, and with relative isolation from the rest of the college community within their own, but is directly related to the life-work of those discriminated against and their opportunity for both professional and social self-realization. Although the Jewish college applicant or undergraduate who is an earnest student is in a critical position regarding his future, it is even worse for the Jewish medical or law student who is four or more years his senior. Thus, the exclusion of competent Jewish applicants from professional schools on discriminatory grounds or discrimination against them after admission touches, so to speak, a very raw nerve.

The quota system of admission in undergraduate schools is an inequity that affects primarily the student discriminated against; the same system applied to candidates in medicine, law, engineering, and accounting represents a distinct calamity for American society. This is particularly true of medicine, a field to which Jews have traditionally been attracted, and in which they have a long history of distinguished activity:

While discussions of the relationship between Judaism and medicine almost always lead to the mention of Maimonides, this relationship is probably as old as the Biblical "I am the Lord, thy Physician" (Exodus 15:26). Some scholars contend that medicine was taught as an independent subject at the Talmudic academies of Babylonia and Palestine; even those who disagree admit that it was a major topic of interest. Certainly by medieval times Judaism and medicine were firmly joined. Cecil Roth, in *The Jewish Contribution to Civilization,* estimates that half of all medieval rabbis were practicing doctors. Throughout the Middle Ages, too, medicine headed the secular curriculum of many Jewish schools.[64]

American Jews have retained this traditional interest in the practice of medicine, even though between 1920 and 1960 there was a decline in the proportion of Jewish students enrolled in medical schools in relation to the total number of Jewish professional students. But the same decline was true for the proportion of all professional students who were studying medicine, since during this period other professions exerted a stronger attraction among the entire population. Yet medicine still stood relatively high among preferred professions:

The occupations specifically mentioned most often by the boys included engineering (21%), business (15%), and medicine (10%). This same choice held for all religious groupings, and the order of preference was the same for Protestants and Catholics. Jewish boys put business (26%) and medicine (19%) well ahead of engineering.[65]

The percentage of Jewish students attending medical schools throughout the United States has remained remarkably stable—an average of between 18 and 19 per cent. There is reason to believe that in an unrestricted situation the proportion would be higher. Certain factors limiting Jewish enrollment in medical schools in some areas and in some schools are clearly not to be ascribed to deliberate anti-Jewish feeling: specifically, the resident requirements of many publicly supported medical schools and the limit on numbers or exclusion of Jews from many church-supported schools. The one medical school under Jewish auspices—the Albert Einstein Medical College of Yeshiva University—does *not* limit or exclude non-Jews, despite its auspices.

In certain areas, notably the Northeast, the proportion of Jewish students has increased considerably in recent years. This seems to point to another factor responsible, at least in part, for the persistence of rigid quotas against Jewish medical students. The quota system is most evident in those parts of the country that lack the Fair Educational Practices legis. lation of states like Massachusetts and New York. This is even more regrettable during the present period when there is a shortage of doctors.

The number of doctors is not keeping pace with our growing population. An advisory committee has reported to Surgeon General Burney that the shortage will become serious unless the number of medical school graduates is raised from the present 7,000 a year (including osteopaths) to 11,000. Otherwise, it says, there will be only 133 doctors for every 100,000 persons by 1975, instead of the present 140.7. This will occur, it says, even if we license 750 foreign medical graduates a year. It urges that the nation launch a billion-dollar program to build 20 to 24 new medical schools and expand the 91 existing ones.[66]

Yet a recent survey by the Anti-Defamation League has shown that potentially discriminatory application forms have caused a bottleneck for medical training. During 1957– 59, a study of the application forms used by the seventy-nine accredited medical schools in the United States indicated that the average application contained 2.4 potentially discriminatory questions—questions whose answers might be used as a basis for discrimination against the applicant on racial or religious grounds.

Considerable progress had indeed been made in the course of the previous decade—many medical schools had dropped such questions. In 1949, the average number of potentially discriminatory questions was 4.29, and *every one* of the sixty-five medical schools surveyed used at least one such question in its application form, while by 1959, seven of the application blanks contained none at all.[67]

An important distinction must be made between blunt questions about an applicant's race or religion and questions which may serve to elicit such information indirectly. Current application forms have many such indirect questions. However construed, they provide the medical schools that do discriminate with a basis on which to practice selectivity related to, if not determined by, prejudice.

The following table lists both indirect and direct potentially discriminatory questions discovered by the Anti-Defamation League in the application forms of seventy-nine medical schools in 1957–58:

Indirect questions	No. of times asked	Direct questions	No. of times asked
Photograph	66	Applicant's Religion	10 (incl. 2 Catholic schools)
Applicant's Birthplace	64	Church Membership	9
Parents' Birthplace	24	Applicant's Race	9 (incl. 2 Negro schools)
Mother's Maiden Name	20	Applicant's Nationality	6
		Parents' Religion	4
		Parents' Nationality	3
		Parents' Race	1

This does not mean that all, or most, medical schools in the United States deliberately restrict their Jewish students. In the first place, as indicated, there has been a strong improvement in application forms. Moreover, there is the previously mentioned geographic factor, which affects all students in the Northeast, not Jewish students alone. According to a 1952 study conducted by the Council of Medical Education of the American Medical Association, 25 per cent of the nation's medical schools barred out-of-state students and more than 50 per cent gave preference to those from their own states. On the other hand, none of New York state's medical schools restricts applicants from other states. As a result, all New York premedical students, of whom a large number are Jewish, are handicapped. Since they are barred from entering many schools in other states, they are forced to compete with applicants from those very states for places in New York's medical colleges.

Nor should it be assumed out of hand that small numbers of Jewish students, or none at all, at a particular medical school necessarily means that anti-Jewish discrimination is being practiced. The ADL medical school surveys for the entering classes of 1956, 1957, and 1958 show that in the Far West fewer than sixty students, 9 per cent of the total admitted, were Jewish. Yet a check of two of the Far Western medical schools revealed no evidence that there was a discriminatory policy directed against Jewish students. A possible explanation of the dearth of Jewish students in these schools was that they are located in areas that have a small Jewish population.

Conversely, a comparatively large number of Jewish students, constituting a relatively high proportion of the student body, does not necessarily connote an unprejudiced attitude toward Jewish medical-school applicants. The New England and North Atlantic regions had the highest number and proportion of Jewish medical students in the entering classes of 1957 and 1958 (between 30 and 33 per cent), yet it is in these regions that evidence exists of deliberate exclusion and restriction of Jewish applicants.

This is illustrated by findings concerning medical school practices in Pennsylvania and New York state. In April 1957 the Philadelphia Fellowship Commission made public the results of a five-year survey based on the experiences of premedical students graduated from the college at the University of Pennsylvania and from the liberal arts school at Temple University. After studying the experiences, personal background, and qualifications of these students, the survey concluded that Catholics had less chance of acceptance than Protestants, and Jews less chance than Catholics. According to the report, religion was the most potent factor in influencing the student's chance of admission:

The applicant of Catholic or Jewish religious background is less likely to be accepted than the applicant of Protestant background. The Jewish applicant is at an even greater disadvantage at this respect. . . . The influence of the applicant's religion on his chances of acceptance appear to cut across all other factors—including school grades, extra-curricular participation, and even his father's occupation.[68]

In 1950 and 1952, two official New York state bodies investigated allegations of New York's discriminatory policies. The State Department of Education's Bienenstok study found that New York medical schools discriminated against Jewish and Italian applicants. In June 1953, the State Board of Regents published the results of its own study of medical-school practices. The Regents confirmed the Department of Education's finding that an applicant's religious background affected his chances of getting into a medical school in New York state.

Both in 1950 and in 1952, it was discovered, Jewish medical-school applicants had the highest average scholastic marks, followed by Protestant and Catholic students. But:

This order does not conform to the order of admission. Top-ranking Protestant and Catholic students are more certain to be admitted than are top-ranking Jewish students; at the other end of his scholastic scale, low-rating Jewish students are virtually excluded while occasionally low-rating Protestant and Catholic applicants are admitted.

What may be expected in the future, on the basis of such reports? We have already cited the national need for physicians and noted how continued prejudice against Jewish medical applicants may deepen the need. The 1957 Philadelphia study presents corroborative data. It notes that Jewish students seem to be accepted in greater numbers when medical schools are faced with a shortage of applicants, but when there is an excess of applicants, the quota system is reinstituted.

The medical-school quota system, although still in operation, has lost some of its virulent character during the past decade. Begun some forty years ago, it reached its peak in the late 1930s and 1940s, and tapered off during the 1950s. In October 1945, it was reported that throughout the United States there had been 794 Jewish medical students in the class of 1937, while in the class of 1940 the number had dropped to 477.[69] By 1958, the number of Jews in the first year of medical school had almost tripled, to 1468.

The future situation is unpredictable. Because of the sharp rise of the American birth rate in the early 1940s, the expectation is that there will be a great increase in the number of medical-school applicants in the 1960s. There is more than a faint possibility, as the Philadelphia study indicates, that medical schools, whose facilities have not kept pace with the increasing demand and need for doctors, may reinstitute or strengthen existing quota systems.

Yet this prediction is not at all certain, since American society is so variable and the conditions of life change rapidly and drastically. It is possible that the quota system may not reappear in the next few years because of the general decline in the proportion of all Jewish students in professional curricula. Jewish medical students, as noted, continue to constitute 18 per cent of the national medical school body. But medicine is only one profession, and for the past three decades Jewish students have shown a decided preference for several other professions that, like medicine, offer opportunities for self-employment and in which probability of economic discrimination is minimized. During this same period, particularly since the end of World War II, there has been a tremendous influx of students into colleges and universities. The growth in national enrollment inevitably has its impact on the number of students who go on to professional curricula. Jewish students have not shared the national trend, for there has been no comparable increase in their numbers. What has taken place, instead, has been a redistribution of Jewish professional students to fields where no quotas exist.

Another factor that explains the decreased proportion of Jewish students to the enrollment as a whole was the increase in the proportion of male students to the total enrollment between 1935 and 1955: males predominate in professional schools.

The gradual broadening of the vocational interests of Jewish youth is also indicated by the fact that in 1957 the largest percentage of all Jewish students reported in any professional curriculum was in business administration—23.6 per cent.[70] This preference is likely to continue. Large numbers of Jews have traditionally been attracted to business, and with the professionalization of business administration more and more young people believe that specific college training is good preparation for business. Accounting, which is largely an independent profession, today represents another expanding field in which it is possible for a young man or woman to carve out a career without having to face serious discriminatory obstacles.

Teaching is next in importance as a goal of Jewish students' professional aspirations—18.9 per cent of all Jewish students in the professional field in 1957 reported they were studying education. In New York City, Jewish students comprised 16 per cent of all students preparing for a teaching career; they were about 6 per cent of all education students in both the New England and the Middle Atlantic regions. Like business and medicine, teaching has deep roots in Jewish tradition and cultural values. During the past twenty years, the prolonged teacher shortage and the lessening of discrimination against Jews in the teaching profession has allowed the classic Jewish cultural pattern of study, scholarship, and instruction as worthwhile ends in themselves to reassert itself. In addition, Jewish students face less heavy competition in the teaching field because it is one of the least remunerative of all the professions. Partly for this reason, schools of education have relaxed religious barriers to a greater extent than other professional schools. They have the lowest figure in the use of discriminatory applications.[71]

Finally, educators tend to take a large view of their social role. In the words of one educator, "Education is a prime way of creating social wealth." The gradual increase in the number of American Jews who aspire to be teachers is probably a conjunction of three factors: First, the Jewish heritage of preoccupation with scholarship and education as a social good. Second, the teacher shortage, accompanied by a decrease in anti-Jewish discrimination. Third, the so-called occupational liberalism of educators.

A third profession into which Jews have lately obtained access in growing numbers is engineering. Here again, the picture is not a simple one. Young Jewish men shy away from civil engineering to some extent, since it does not offer the same opportunities for advancement and self-employment as are available to those who choose the electrical or chemical branches. The latter two branches are growing most rapidly, another factor that has attracted Jewish youth. Discrimination has tended to adhere to the older branches of engineering, where it had its original roots.

The future for Jewish professionals in engineering is uncertain but far from hopeless. Presumably, in view of the national concentration on scientific achievement, there will continue to be a need for trained engineers and engineering technicians. (Nevertheless, in 1960 there was the beginning of a decline in enrollment in engineering schools for the first time in seven years.)[72]

In any event, graduate enrollment in engineering has reached new peaks, and the number of degrees awarded in engineering continued to rise at all levels (undergraduate, master, doctor). It is too soon to speculate just how this will affect potential Jewish engineers.

CHAPTER 12

The System Is Changing

●

The half-way point in the four-year life of the National Defense Education Act of 1958 was marked last week with a report on the present status of its provisions. Out of the total $1 billion authorized by the act, Congress has so far appropriated more than $275 million.

Student Loans: About $70 million has been allocated to 1,197 institutions for 27,683 approved loans in 1959, and to 360 institutions for 150,000 approved loans for 1960. It is estimated that 1,450 institutions will receive about $61 million for 175,000 loans in 1961. The N.D.E.A. loans approved during the past school year amount to at least four times more than was loaned in 1955–56 by all colleges.

Science, Mathematics and Foreign Language Instruction: Over $102 million has been allocated to the states for acquisition of equipment and remodeling of facilities in these areas of instruction.

National Defense Fellowships: To meet the growing shortage of college teachers, 2,500 graduate fellowships have been awarded, 1,500 of them for study beginning next fall.

—*The New York Times,* June 26, 1960

The Federal Government is deeply involved financially in the higher education of its citizens. Its expenditure for general support of colleges and universities; for aid to students, teachers, and institutions for specific educational programs; and for research in or by colleges and universities is estimated to be $1.5 to $2 billion a year.

Insofar as applicants to publicly controlled colleges and universities are denied admission on such arbitrary grounds as their race, religion, or national origin, they not only are denied equal protection of the laws under the Constitution, but also are denied the opportunity to participate, directly or indirectly, in the benefits resulting from the use by such institutions of Federal funds.

Insofar as the Federal Government, whether by allotment, grant, or contract, disburses funds to publicly controlled colleges and universities practicing racial exclusion, whether of Negro students or white, it is supporting operations in violation of the Constitution.

The Supreme Court has held that the Federal Government is prohibited by the Constitution from maintaining racially segregated educational institutions. It is not sound policy for the Federal Government to subsidize the unconstitutional operations of others; to do indirectly what it is not permitted to do directly.

It is not a sound policy for the Federal Government to disburse public funds in such a manner that it increases the adverse effects on some citizens of denials of equal protection of the laws by states and political subdivisions thereof. . . .

Therefore, the commission recommends that the Federal Government, either by executive or, if necessary, by Congressional action, take such measures as may be required to assure that funds under the various programs of Federal assistance to higher education are disbursed only to such publicly controlled institutions of higher education as do not discriminate on grounds of race, color, religion, or national origin.

—Excerpts from reports of the
Federal Civil Rights Commission
issued January 16, 1961

A number of noteworthy developments within the past generation presage a radical change in the American educational system in general and colleges and universities in particular. Such a change has already affected discriminatory patterns. Other changes may be anticipated that are so drastic as to alter completely the targets, if not the operations, of discrimination.

We have noted earlier the intense responsiveness of American society to alterations in the national economy—in reaction to the country's material needs, population has been redistributed, social classes shuffled, and immigrant groups absorbed in different manners. This is not to deprecate the role of basic American ideas, but these ideas have been modified—interpreted widely or restrictively, stressed for their conservative or their liberal elements—to adjust to new technological developments. Insofar as American society is a classic open society, its educational institutions have at different periods changed their structure for the purpose of maintaining that openness. In the words of George Z. F. Bereday:

By keeping the flow of mobility free from barriers of birth, wealth, and other types of discrimination, and by reducing social distance through social and occupational upgrading of the majority, the American common school has had its part in creating a surprisingly egalitarian and homogeneous society.[73]

These words refer to elementary rather than to higher education. Dr. Bereday further comments that "education has become a field of social discrimination." Nevertheless, American colleges and universities *have* moved with the times. "In an industrial, functional, increasingly professional age, the distinctions of intellect have long tended to replace the distinctions of birth and wealth that preceded them."

It is important in charting the course of discrimination in higher education to review the history of American universities and colleges. That history reflects the diversity and variety of American life:

> In the United States the word "university" has been applied to institutions of the most diverse character. . . . Harvard, William and Mary, and Yale, the three pioneers of colonial times, were organized in the days of colonial poverty, on the plans of the English colleges which constitute the universities of Oxford and Cambridge. . . . The underlying principle in these institutions was discipline—mental, moral and religious. Dormitories and commons were provided, and attendance upon religious worship in the chapel was enforced. . . . Around or near these *nuclei,* during the course of the 19th century, one or more professional schools were frequently attached, and so the word "university" was naturally applied to a group of schools associated more or less closely with a central school or "college." . . . The ecclesiastic, or religious, note was a strong characteristic of these foundations. . . . In the oldest and largest colleges this denominational influence has ceased to have the importance it once possessed.
>
> Noteworthy innovations came when Thomas Jefferson, the philosophical statesman, returned to the United States from France. . . . He led the Virginians to establish, on a new plan, the University of Virginia . . . ; the freshness of his advice, the importation of distinguished foreign teachers, and the freedom of the student from an enforced curriculum . . . led to broad conceptions of academic work. . . . Following Virginia's example, many of the new states in the West established state universities. . . . Freedom from ecclesiastic control is found in all the foundations that make up this second group—the state universities. . . .
>
> Since 1865 another class of universities has arisen, quite distinct from the colonial establishments and from the wards of the states. These are independent foundations due to individual generosity. The gifts of Johns Hopkins, Rockefeller (University of Chicago), Tulane, De Pauw, Clark and Leland Stanford brought into being universities which have no dependence upon state control . . . and when a denominational character is assured this fact is not made prominently.
>
> Thus, looking at their origin, we see three impulses given to

American high schools, from churches, states, and individuals. . . . Another influence, proceeding from the national government, must also be borne in mind. During the Civil War, Congress . . . bestowed upon every state a certain portion of the public domain in the Far West—"landscrip," as it was called—the proceeds of its sale to be devoted to the establishment and maintenance of one or more colleges in each state, where instruction should be given in agriculture and the mechanic arts, not excluding liberal studies, and including military tactics. In some states this bounty was directed to existing institutions. . . . While all these schools were regarded as practical and technical at the first, most of them as they developed became liberal and scientific.

This sketch would not be complete without the mention of two foundations, each unique. The Catholic University in Washington has been created by the Pope, and in its government the hierarchy of the Roman Catholic Church is made dominant. . . . The newer metropolitan university was distinctly organized on a broader plan, in closer accordance with the universities of continental Europe, and with a pronounced recognition of the importance of science. The University of the State of New York is a supervisory (not a teaching) body exercising a general control over all the schools of higher instruction of the state, and especially guarding the conditions upon which degrees are conferred.[74]

In the half-century since the summary above was written, higher education in the United States has expanded considerably. It has responded to various and—sometimes—conflicting influences. Progressive education has left its mark in the work-study program at such colleges as Antioch and Bennington. A contrasting "great books" program has been stressed at St. John's College (Md.) and the University of Chicago. There has been ardent concentration on scientific and technological scholarship and research at such schools as the Massachusetts Institute of Technology and California Institute of Technology. And, during the last few decades, government and sectarian groups have expanded educational institutions to meet particular needs.

Each of these developments has been part of the threefold stream of American education outlined a half-century earlier; denomination-, state-, and individual-inspired.

In what manner have these developments affected educational opportunities for American Jews—and how may they affect those opportunities in the future?

Even those colleges and universities that are under denominational auspices no longer stress sectarianism to the exclusion of extrasectarian students. Brandeis University and Yeshiva University's Albert Einstein College of Medicine, both under Jewish auspices, admit students regardless of "race, nationality, religion, and ethnic background." Brandeis has symbolized this open policy by building three religious chapels—for Protestants, Catholics, and Jews. The Albert Einstein College of Medicine is one of the institutions that lists no potentially discriminatory questions whatsoever on its application blanks. In both these schools, there is, understandably, a preponderance of Jews. At Fordham, Notre Dame, and St. John's, among other Catholic institutions, there is no quota against Jewish students. Obviously, these denominationally based schools provide special opportunity for students of their own denomination to practice their faith, but there is no pressure on other students to conform—and certainly no prejudicial treatment.

An even greater contribution to the changing educational scene is the proliferation of local and regional colleges and the increasing attraction of metropolitan universities. The city colleges are free, with no restrictions beyond residence and scholarship. Junior colleges, a more recent innovation, are two-year schools stressing, usually, a vocational curriculum. After graduation, students may transfer to a four-year college or university or go out into the world with their junior-college diploma. Both city and junior colleges reflect the demand for a novel kind of institution—one firmly based in a large urban community where the students live and directly influenced by the demands of that community.

The implications for discrimination against Jewish students of what may be called the "metropolitanization of higher education" may indeed be revolutionary. The growth of these schools is part of a general national pattern, closely tied to the larger developing patterns of American society. The residential, dormitory type of self-contained college or university was typical of a rural society, where mobility was limited and students forced to travel hundreds of miles from small communities and settle for four years away from home at the university or college town. Only there could they receive the benefit of wider intellectual and cultural stimuli indispensable to a truly free and broad education. The university was a special universe in miniature, and extension of London, Paris, Athens, and New York. It was a kind of spiritual haven for pilgrims from the hinterlands.

With the industrialization of America, with the increased mobility afforded by the automobile and excellent public transportation, and with the present urban concentration of population, there has been a transformation of American society—and of higher education. The current trend is for students to live at home and commute to large metropolitan schools, sometimes for a distance of as much as fifty miles. The students thus have the best of two worlds: the world of the university, with its specialized, professional scholarship, and the world of urban culture, with its unparalleled opportunities for both learning and recreation.

What this means for prospective Jewish students is that they are no longer bound by the economics of higher education to live within the relatively rigid confines of campus society, no longer dependent on dormitories for living quarters and on fraternities or sororities for sharply stratified personal associations. The large city or junior college and the metropolitan university make it possible for the Jewish student to avoid the small-town college situation that many times fostered discrimination in housing and personal relations.

Finally, the federal government's active aid to universities and colleges, particularly for scientific research, and the scholarships that both the government and industry have given to superior students have opened more opportunities for able Jewish students. These grants are untainted by prejudice.

In general, one may say that the development of higher education in the United States has been away from exclusiveness as a result of the open-enrollment policy of the nondenominational schools, the establishment of new regional colleges, and the expansion of city and junior colleges.

The situation has been improving, and the prospects for continued improvement seem good. Yet prejudice is not easily eliminated. Neither the lower cost of education nor an increase in facilities will automatically eliminate prejudice. However, they will blunt the edge of discrimination.[75]

To "blunt the edge" of discrimination remains the practical problem.

IV. DISCRIMINATION IN EMPLOYMENT

CHAPTER 13. **Sorry, the Job Is Filled**

●

Example

"Protestants only, no Jews or Orientals."

"We have no religious preferences as long as they are of the Nordic race."

"This is a Gentile firm; a Jewish girl wouldn't be comfortable here."

"We're desperate, but not desperate enough to hire Jews."

"We can't use any of the forbidden race."

"We only employ high type Anglo-Saxons."

—from the files of Chicago employment agencies

Some of the terms used on employment-agency job orders or application blanks are *All American* and *G*, which stand for white Gentiles only. *Ivy League type* is often used on the East Coast, *Nordic* in Chicago. They mean the same thing.

A West Coast employment agency will note on its job orders *No O's*, *No Sp's*, and *C*, meaning no Orientals, no Mexican-Americans, and Caucasians only. A more guarded system is used by some East Coast agencies: *1* means that an applicant is white, *2* that he is Negro, *3* that he is Spanish-

American or Puerto Rican, and *1–3* that he is white but Puerto Rican. The same employment agencies use the label *No Sabbath Observer* to indicate that Jews are not wanted.

The code designations frequently have no apparent connection with logic. An imaginative private New York agency uses *Recommended by Redbook* on a job order to indicate that Negroes are not wanted, *Must play saxophone* to indicate that Jews need not apply, and *U.S. Citizen* to indicate the exclusion of Puerto Ricans—who are, of course, citizens.

Policies of discrimination in employment are laid down by employers, not by employment agencies. Nonetheless, there are a number of persons who believe that this should not absolve the employment agency that collaborates with bigoted employers.

These people believe that by accepting and handling discriminatory job orders, the employment agency agrees to do the dirty work of such employers. The agency serves as a protective curtain by affording the firm anonymity and shielding it from public exposure. Willingness to go along with this can be ascribed in part to the single-minded attitude of most employment-agency operators. As they see it, their role is simply to provide a service and collect a fee. It was summed up by one operator, who said to an ADL staff member:

"We get paid when we send an employer what he wants. I don't care if a person has green skin and two heads; if an employer wanted such a person and I could find him, I'd certainly refer him to the firm."

We all know that there is employment discrimination against Negroes and Puerto Ricans. But is there *really* discrimination against Jews in employment in the United States, or is this merely another bogey raised by "hypersensitive, thin-skinned" American Jews?

On the whole Jews are well off economically in this country. For example, in Detroit, during the 1951–54 period the average annual income for heads of Jewish households was $6200, considerably higher than the average for the rest of the community. The author of a statistical work previously cited implies that American Jews have no reason to complain:

Are the members of any religious group discriminated against, in their efforts to find employment, simply because of their particular religious preference? One might conclude that they are if, in any religious group, the household heads have jobs that are low in the socio-economic scale, and levels of educational attainment that are extraordinarily high. . . . Three groups fit this pattern: the Presbyterian, the Methodist, and the Episcopal. If the data are accepted as valid, one would be forced to conclude that the Episcopal group is more severely discriminated against than any other. Common-sense reflection suggests that this is not the case; if there is discrimination of the type defined above, it should show up among the Baptists, a group having a very large Negro population. Probably nothing more is involved than the fact that Episcopalians, Presbyterians, and Methodists place a stronger emphasis on educational achievement than many other religious groups do, and hence, that their members tend to attain above-average educational levels irrespective of the occupational levels at which they may eventually work. To summarize: the meager data available gives little evidence either that any religious group is extraordinarily favored, or that there is severe discrimination (independent of any other factors) against any religious group because of its beliefs—with respect to broad categories of occupational attainment. Although the religious groups differ substantially with respect to occupational composition, in general the members of each religion seem to be located just about as high on the occupational ladder as the level of their educational attainment would lead one to expect.[76]

But take American Jews, not mentioned in this quotation, as an example. It is not that they have had little difficulty in achieving their present socio-economic status, but that they have *overcome* those difficulties through extraordinary exertions. For instance, (Jewish applicants have been denied admission to medical schools far more often than comparably qualified non-Jewish students, but they have persisted in applying to many more schools until they found one that would admit them. The end result is that both Jews and non-Jews who have graduated from medical schools practice their profession, and the statistics show a clear relationship between the cause (professional training) and the effect (higher socio-economic status). However, the middle term—the *process*—has been omitted. It is the *process* American Jews refer to when they speak of anti-Semitic discrimination in employment.)

The same author also undertakes to prove that religious affiliation is of very little importance in accounting for differences between the incomes of members of different religious groups *with the same education:*

It should not be concluded hastily that any of the socio-economic differences shown here are due directly to religious membership as such. The kind of occupational use to which a given amount of educational attainment is put has a great deal to do with the amount of income received. People with college degrees who choose law, medicine, or business administration as a career (as a high proportion of Jewish and Episcopal members do), and who have spent 5 to 8 years in college, will almost certainly receive much larger incomes than other college graduates who have spent 4 years in college and have chosen to teach elementary school or to hold other kinds of low-paying jobs as professionals or officials. Moreover, persons who live in large metropolitan areas (as a high proportion of Jews and Episcopalians do) receive higher incomes for a given occupation than workers living in other places. To summarize: *education is a much more potent factor than religious preference in determining the income level of households,* and even observed differences between religious groups, when amount of education is controlled, may be due to "intervening variables" other than religious affiliation.[77]

Quite possibly this analyst has been misled by his appreciation of the fact that economic discrimination in the United States is directed mainly against nonwhites, principally the Negro. American Negroes have been so restricted in their educational opportunities that their economic advancement has been retarded, and their low income level reflects their limited job possibilities. But neither of these criteria of discrimination applies to Jews. It is false to assert that because Jews are well educated, include a large proportion of professionals, and have a relatively high income, they are not subjected to economic discrimination, even though it is not so severe as the economic discrimination against Negroes and takes somewhat different forms.

It is necessary to refer to factors other than education and income to evaluate employment discrimination against Jews in the United States at this time. The first point to note is economic concentration. Is the Jewish occupational pattern askew because of a concentration in certain trades, professions, industries?

Undoubtedly, American Jews *are* concentrated in certain economic areas and occupations. It does not follow automatically, however, that this concentration is unhealthy either for the Jewish group or for the national economy. For example, the United States needs physicians, and it should make no difference whether they are Jews or Christians.

Likewise, it does not automatically follow that this kind of concentration is peculiar to Jews in the United States. Economic concentration is bound to be true of any group of the total population which is relatively small (the Jews constitute some 3.5 per cent), and whose arrival in the United States was concentrated during a relatively short span of time (the period between 1880 and 1920 for American Jewish immigrants). Members of such a group must quickly find employment, and to do so they seek out co-religionists or fellow members of their cultural group. This is a general pattern, seen also among immigrants from Italy and Ireland who arrived in equally large numbers at the same time as the Jews.

Although the general pattern of concentration is true of all immigrant groups, *where* a particular, new immigrant group will concentrate economically depends on two other factors: the character of the group on its arrival, and the economic opportunities in the country at that time.

A study of foreign-born Jews in the United States in 1920 revealed they were primarily urban. This town origin was reflected in the immigrant's occupational distribution. As W. L. Warner and L. Srole have pointed out, those ethnic groups which have been urban for the longest period of time seem to have an occupational distribution that is more heavily weighted in the professional, clerical class than those groups whose urban experience is more recent.[78] Though the urban history of the Jewish immigrants was small-town or village rather than metropolitan, because of residential restrictions in eastern Europe that excluded most Jews from large settlements, Jewish religious culture was essentially urban in temperament. Their stress on rationality, prudence, saving, and sobriety helped prepare them psychologically for the competitiveness and other adaptations peculiar to city life, as well as for the moderate middle-class values of the New World. This cultural-religious past is what sociologists refer to as a fixed factor in a group's experience.

In the case of the Jews, their urban background of group-preserving values proved a distinct asset in their accommodation to an American society that was growing more and more urban and security-centered. As a group, the Jewish immigrants could readily feel they *belonged* in America. They could respond with relative directness to the problem of occupational adjustment, because their group value system, inherited and learned, was oriented in the same direction as the general American value system. Since occupational adjustment is a major aspect of group life, the original concentration of the Jewish immigrants in certain industries and occupations was a happy as well as a natural one—it had the approbation both of the smaller group and of the larger society. The values and background the Jewish immigrants brought with them to the United States help explain their occupational concentration.

What were the economic conditions when the group arrived? And how did those conditions influence the immigrants' choice of employment? During the period of the heaviest Jewish immigration, nonmanual occupations were expanding greatly in the United States, while unskilled manual labor and farming were employing a progressively smaller proportion of the labor force. (Between 1910 and 1950, for example, the proportion of the American population engaged in nonmanual work rose from 21 per cent to 38 per cent.) Since the Jewish immigrants had pronounced urban and middle-class tendencies, it was inevitable that, as a group, they would move quickly out of manual occupations into commerce and the professions.

This situation offered a unique opportunity to a group of immigrants who, like the Jews, were socially, culturally, and psychologically equipped to take advantage of it. (It should be noted, however, that manual labor was not beneath the dignity of eastern-European Jews. There were many Jewish tailors, shoemakers, porters. The Jewish socialist movement was based on an active industrial proletariat, particularly class-conscious in Poland between the two World Wars. Yet, traditionally, the People of the Book esteemed intellectual labor more highly than physical labor.)

With this background, the Jewish immigrants and their children were well equipped to more than hold their own in America. A study of New Haven during the 1940s led observers to the conclusion that Jews, in fact, improved on their initial advantage. While they had a slight superiority in terms of occupational status and urban skills to Italian immigrants on their arrival during the period between 1910 and 1939, the original advantage widened appreciably. By 1940, Jews consistently had higher occupational status than the average of the New Haven population. In contrast, Italians who arrived in New Haven at the same time had a consistently lower average occupational status than Jews.[79]

Our summary to this point has revealed no prejudice against Jews so damaging as to cripple their struggle for economic status.

However, *nonmanual occupations* is a very large term. In what particular nonmanual occupations have American Jews tended to concentrate—and in what particular industries? Within these industries and occupations are the Jews subject to restrictions as to hiring, salary, promotion, and clientele in comparison with other groups or the population as a whole? These are the key questions for an appreciation of the nuances of anti-Jewish employment discrimination in the United States.

Data in the 1950 census show that Jews were more highly represented in the wholesale-retail trades than in manufacturing. There was also a fairly heavy Jewish participation in real estate and insurance, but as agents or free-lancers rather than full members of the company staff. Occupationally, a much larger proportion of the Jewish labor force was in the professional and managerial group than was true of the general American population; a smaller percentage of Jews were in skilled and semi-skilled occupations. Population studies of Jewish communities made within the past fifteen

years show that about one third of gainfully employed Jews
may be classed as professionals, proprietors, managers, and
officials; slightly more than a third are clerical workers; about
one tenth are skilled workers; and about one fifth are classed
as semi-skilled and unskilled workers.⟩

Does this rough description jibe with the apprehensions
over an "abnormal" concentration of Jews in the trades and
professions? It is like taking literally the idea of the "average
American" as the norm. An average, a norm, is useful only
for purposes of comparison or as a statistical device. It is
not intended to be adapted to pejorative ends. It is helpful
to compare Jewish occupational and industrial statistics with
that of the "general population," because such a comparison
helps to define what is characteristic of American Jews. But
it must be remembered that the "average American" is even
more of an abstraction than the "average Jew." If underprivileged groups such as Negroes, Puerto Ricans, Mexicans
were omitted, Jewish economic progress would be less striking. And if Jews were compared with high-status older immigrant groups rather than with their contemporaries in immigration and original status, the concentration of Jews in
certain occupations would be less unusual. For example:

Three religions stand out distinctively as having large percentages
of their groups in "white-collar" employment: the Episcopal, the
Jewish, and the Presbyterian. Of these three, the Episcopal group
contains the largest percentage of professional and technical persons, while the Jewish group has substantial proportions in managerial and proprietary jobs.

Occupational Composition of Household Heads, by Religious Affiliation

Religious Affil.	Professional technical	Office and Managerial Proprietary	Clerical	Sales
Presbyterian	15.3	16.1	8.2	10.6
Episcopal	19.6	20.4	11.0	5.4
Jewish	17.6	36.0	9.6	15.0[80]

At first glance it appears that within this occupational classification American Presbyterians, Episcopalians, and Jews must have certain features in common, such as a drive for education and residence in larger metropolitan areas where education can be put to practical use most easily. However, upon close examination, it is clear that the proportion of Jews in the "office, managerial, proprietary" column equals the combined proportions of Presbyterians and Episcopalians and almost equals them in the "sales" column.

Mathematically significant, even after discounting the percentage of Jews who naturally gravitated to pursuits where other Jews had already established themselves, these figures are important historically. They reflect century-old reluctance to grant Jews the right to work in certain occupations and industries, a consequent crowding of Jews into certain economic positions, and a reaction on the part of Jews resulting from a drive to develop a "normal" economic base for the Jewish group as a whole within the larger national economy. However, all this does not justify the fear some have of Jewish overconcentration in certain occupations and trades. It is an irrational fear, in terms of the objective situation and must be understood as part of a present ideological situation.

Ideology aside, the Jewish occupational pattern is traceable to three factors. Two of these factors—history and education—have already been mentioned. The third factor is place of residence. Here, too, the widespread picture of the big-city Jew requires modification. American Jews do not live only in very large cities such as New York City but also in small and medium-sized communities. Moreover, there is a significant difference in their employment situation depending on the size of the urban community. Outside New York, where some 40 per cent of the American Jewish population does reside, the Jewish working force falls into expected major groupings. However, in New York City the order of occupational groupings is somewhat different:

outside New York	*within New York*
1. Proprietors and managers	1. Clerical and sales
2. Clerical and sales workers	2. Skilled and unskilled workers
3. Professionals	ers
4. Skilled and unskilled workers	3. Proprietors and managers
ers	4. Professionals.

Another difference between Jews who live in New York City and those who live in smaller urban communities is in self-employment. Outside New York, anywhere from 50 to 70 per cent of Jewish professionals are self-employed. But in New York City only about a third of the professionals are self-employed, while some 63 per cent are either privately employed or in government service.

Why are these statistics important?

There is a tendency among both Jews and non-Jews to exaggerate the concentration of Jews in executive positions in business and in the professions. This is so because the Jewish proportion in these occupations is viewed in relation to the general population, not in relation to the comparable proportion of other groups or the Jewish group as a whole. Thus, in New York City, where Jews add up to just over a quarter of the city's population, they constitute more than 45 per cent of the proprietor and managerial category and 33 per cent of the professional and semiprofessional categories.[81] In the country as a whole, the Jews are more heavily represented in the professional and proprietorial categories than the average. But as noted above, it is more accurate to compare the Jewish occupational pattern with groups having a similar educational background rather than with a heterogeneous "average."

Henry Cohen points out (in a 1955 report on New York

Jews for the New York Federation of Jewish Philanthropies) that in general there is the same proportion of males in the Jewish group's working force as there is in the population of the city at large. However, the Jewish working force has a different age distribution than the general New York City working force. There is a smaller proportion of employed Jews between the ages of fourteen and twenty-one than the proportion of workers of the same age in the city as a whole. This is counterbalanced by the higher proportion of employed Jewish males over twenty-five.

Again, this reflects a Jewish concentration in professional and managerial occupations—which requires that they spend their late teens and early twenties receiving advanced education that they compensate for by continuing their careers longer than relatively untrained workers—a pattern that holds for all groups with the same occupational interests as American Jews.

Thus, another significant average—age—is often overlooked by those who view with alarm the representation of Jews in certain occupations. Jews as a group apparently have a higher average age than their colleagues. It is also known that the older age groups in this country tend to have higher proportions of professionals, semiprofessionals, proprietors, managers, and officials. In these "intellectual" occupations, too, income tends to increase with education, age, and experience, whereas in occupations requiring less training and more physical skills, income tends to decrease with age. Thus, the more mature a physician the more highly he is respected and the higher the fee he commands, while a factory worker may slow down after he passes his fortieth birthday.

What is also significant in the pattern of occupation of the whole Jewish labor force is the considerable number and proportion of Jews in the nonprofessional white collar and in the skilled and unskilled occupations. In New York the nonprofessional and skilled and unskilled Jewish workers are actually more important numerically and proportionately than the professional and managerial, despite the prominence of Jews in the latter two groupings relative to the city population as a whole.

Another factor that should also be considered has to do with the industrial classification of Jews in the United States. All the figures indicate a predilection on the part of the Jewish labor force for the wholesale and retail trades. But it has been suggested that the emphasis on trades among the Jews tends to decline in the larger population and industrial centers such as New York. In several other communities where some great manufacturing industry dominates the economic and social life of the town, a fairly large proportion of the Jewish labor force, together with general labor, will be found to be part of the community's industrial organization. This is true of Worcester, Newark, Detroit, Passaic, Atlanta, Newark, and Norwich, for instance, as well as New York.

It is often assumed that next to the trades American Jews are most heavily represented in the professions. However, the New York pattern shows not only larger proportions of Jews working as salespeople and skilled and unskilled workers, but it also reveals that they are involved to an unexpected extent in manufacturing. In what branches of manufacturing will be explored at length later, for it is intimately bound with the restriction of Jewish workers.

The question to be pursued first is the reason for discrimination practiced not against Jews who have higher status and more affluence, but against those who have little status or affluence.

In certain urban areas, particularly the very large cities, discrimination against Jewish clerks and sales personnel can be critical for the Jewish population as a whole. This is so not because it pauperizes those discriminated against, but because it isolates a large group of Jewish workers within "Jewish" industries. The problem is rendered even more difficult because of the existence of certain stereotypes of the Jewish worker widely held by both Jews and non-Jews. We refer first, to the notion that the American Jew is only—or at least primarily—interested in commercial or professional work and, second, to the corollary notion that Jews quickly tend to become discontented with private employment at nonprofessional white collar, or even skilled and semi-skilled, jobs because these do not afford the opportunity for extremely rapid advancement.

Employers frequently resort to these notions to justify discriminatory practices against Jews who apply for such jobs. Perhaps unconsciously accepting this evaluation of their own characteristics—at very least as an assumption employers make—Jews who might be expected to apply for such jobs in non-Jewish firms apply instead to Jewish firms. Thus Jewish workers reinforce an undesirable stereotype. Yet, as the data show, many Jews accept and are content with lower status and lower-paying jobs in the economy.

But exactly *where* in the economy?

Mention has been made of the importance of understanding the Jewish industrial concentration as a consequence, at least in some measure, of occupational discrimination. Data on industrial classification emphasize that the Jewish labor force in the United States is concentrated in the wholesale and retail trades. In most of the Jewish communities, the proportion of Jewish workers in the area of commerce ranges from a third in the larger Jewish communities to half in the smaller ones. When the wholesale and retail trades are analyzed, it appears that the major Jewish concentrations are in food establishments, apparel and shoes, and furniture and hardware.

Another significant fact that emerges from such a break-down is that in most of the Jewish communities the proportion of Jews engaged in trade who are in specifically retail enterprises is about 75 per cent. In the United States as a whole, retail trades make up about 85 per cent of the wholesale-retail classification.[82] The stereotype of American Jew as shopkeeper (with its hint of relative "unproductivity" *vis-à-vis* the more "productive" wholesaler), then, is as false as many similar stereotypes.

Finally, analysis of Jewish industrial concentration underlines the Jewish tendency to self-employment, caused *in part* by the response to occupational discrimination. In most of the Jewish communities, there is a noticeable lack of spread among the various industrial classifications. It has been mentioned that in the smaller Jewish communities—New Orleans, for example—as much as half of the Jewish labor force is in the wholesale-retail trades, but this figure increases to almost 70 per cent when Jewish professionals are included.

What these two classifications—sales and the professions—have in common is that they both offer greater opportunities for self-employment than other kinds of industry. Fully 62 per cent of the Jewish males in New Orleans who were engaged in wholesale-retail trades and in professional services were self-employed.

To what extent is this concentration of American Jews in certain occupations and industries a purely voluntary choice, and to what extent does it reflect discriminatory practices in employment and industry?

It is difficult to document the charge of active prejudice with any thoroughness or precision. First, the very motivation for such documentation is weak if not completely missing: the economic well-being of American Jews tends to vitiate moral indignation. Yet anti-Jewish discrimination does exist and its effects, though not crucial to the economic security of Jews, are nevertheless perceptible and meaningful. The experiences of thousands of Jews who encounter prejudicial treatment in their efforts to secure appropriate employment, training, recognition, and advancement in certain occupations and industries leave their marks on their attitudes toward America and toward themselves.

The second difficulty in documenting discrimination against Jews in employment is that, though widespread, it is both subtle and selective. Thus, many firms employ Jews in certain departments and not in others, or assign them certain posts while consciously and rigorously excluding them from others. In some engineering firms, a Jew may rise to the dignity of department head, but the likelihood of his advancing to a front-office job is remote. A real estate or insurance firm may employ Jews as salesmen but less freely in the home office.

The consequence of this selective and subtle pattern is that it is difficult to document economic discrimination against Jews—the firms involved can always point to the employment of Jews in certain capacities while denying any discriminatory intent in their nonemployment. in other capacities. Moreover, as in the case of education, housing, and personal associations, American Jews adopt compensatory devices that tend both to mask and apparently to justify prejudice. As the individual Jewish university student works harder to meet the tougher educational competition he must face, so the individual Jewish worker, restricted in possibilities of employment, works harder to survive the tougher economic barriers. For this he earns the charge of overambition, aggressiveness, dissatisfaction with a middle-level role—in a word, nonconformity.

Another distortion that flows from restriction of opportunity is the suppression of native talents in favor of specious ones. By dint of application, an individual Jew may go far as a salesman in a department store, but if his true inclination lies in another occupation—say medicine—and discrimination has prevented him from realizing that inclination, this causes certain psychological if not material damage, for the deepest needs of his personality are being frustrated. Or if an individual Jew can find employment only in a firm owned by his co-religionists, he may with some justice come to regard all of the United States as being divided into two parts: the Jewish and the non-Jewish. Isolated in the Jewish world, he further isolates himself from American society in his personal associations.

Even though it is difficult to dig beneath the layers of cause, effect, and countereffect, some basic facts about discrimination against Jews in employment have been gathered. One particularly revealing set of data was developed by the Anti-Defamation League concerning the American life insurance industry, and it is worthy of examination in depth as a classic example of the employment problem confronting Jews on the executive level in American big business.

The League embarked on this one-year study in 1959 because it had long been believed that insurance companies did not give equal treatment in employment opportunities to Jews. As long ago as 1936, *Fortune* magazine did a research study on the subject "Jews in America." One conclusion by *Fortune* was: "The absence of Jews in the insurance business is noteworthy."

Although over the years ADL had received documentation of individual instances of discrimination against Jews in the insurance business, there was no over-all data that could serve as a basis for examining the extent of the employment of Jews in this industry. Though it had also been long believed that life insurance companies avoided Jews in executive and administrative positions—particularly in the home offices—it seemed indisputable that over the years Jews have been well represented in the selling ranks.

A major roadblock in establishing the truth or falsity of the belief regarding executive and administrative positions had been the fact that until 1959 no means existed, to the League's knowledge, for determining how many Jews and how many Christians were employed by the insurance companies and in what kinds of job they were. But in that year, ADL obtained from official public records the executive rosters of seven major national life insurance companies that were responsible for more than 50 per cent of the life insurance sales throughout the United States in 1958. The rosters listed by name every salaried employee of these companies who, in the year 1957, received compensation of $10,000 or more. There was a total of 6100 such employees in the lists.

These lists, covering the entire United States, were broken down geographically. The Anti-Defamation League's twenty-six regional office staffs were requested to make a careful determination of Jews and non-Jews. In making these identifications, the ADL staff received the assistance of knowledgeable men and women in the insurance world, thus insuring a maximum of accuracy. In many instances, several sources of information were used to eliminate possible error.

As a consequence of this examination, ADL found that it was unable to identify as Christian *or* Jewish only thirty-four of the 6100 listed executives in home offices and sales branches. In short, ADL's study encompassed 6066 executives throughout the nation, almost 100 per cent of the list. In terms of total staff employment, the companies surveyed included two large, three medium-size, and two relatively small firms.

Of the 6066 executives on the nationwide staffs of the seven life insurance companies, 327, or 5.4 per cent, were Jewish. The company-by-company breakdown of the 6066 executives, analyzing their religious affiliations, follows:

Insurance Company	Number of Executives	Number of Christians	Number of Jews	Pct. of Jews
A	1290	1207	83	6.4
B	2570	2421	149	5.8
C	720	679	41	5.7
D	474	450	24	5.1
E	282	269	13	4.6
F	621	604	17	2.7
G	109	109	0	0.0
Totals	6066	5739	327	5.4

Because there was a question for many years whether Jews were restricted against employment in the home offices of insurance companies, an analysis of ADL's data was made in order to shed light on this issue. (Nonhome-office installations are normally sales offices.) ADL found that of a total of 2020 executives in the home offices of the seven companies, 73, or 3.6 per cent, were of the Jewish faith. In the nonhome-office installations of the seven companies, 6.2 per cent of a total of 4046 individuals so employed throughout the country were of the Jewish faith.

The concentration of Jewish executives, mostly in sales functions, in four states with extremely large Jewish populations is not, according to well-informed sources, the result of happenstance. They say it flows from a design on the part of the insurance companies to hire and place Jewish personnel usually in those areas where the absence of Jewish personnel might have adverse public-relations connotations and where it is calculated that Jewish personnel can enhance the amount of insurance sold to Jews. The point is borne out when one examines the numbers of Jewish executives in communities with small Jewish populations. Thus in St. Louis, which had a Jewish population of 55,000, out of thirty-four executives employed by the insurance companies, only one was Jewish; in the twin cities of St. Paul and Minneapolis, with a combined Jewish population of 33,000, one out of fifty executives was Jewish; in Denver, with a Jewish population of 18,000, there were no Jews among the thirty-one executives; and in Indianapolis, with 8000 Jews, there were no Jews among the twenty-three executives.

The League then examined the job classifications of the 327 Jewish executives. It found only seventy-three Jewish executives employed in the home-office headquarters of six companies. Most of these were clustered in actuarial, medical, legal, and accounting functions.

The remaining 254 Jewish personnel were employed outside the home-office headquarters. Of this number, 236 were employed in branches and agencies concerned primarily with a selling function. These positions carry such job titles as Agency Manager, Associate Manager, Assistant Manager, Manager, Staff Manager—all functions involving the supervision of sales personnel and often including direct contact with the insurance-buying public. It should be noted in this regard that of all Jews employed outside the home-office headquarters, 93 per cent are represented in the classifications that supervised sales personnel.

The League also analyzed the occupations of the non-Jews working outside the home-office headquarters and found that 73.9 per cent of these were in positions where they supervised the selling of insurance. While the actual number of Christians in sales positions was numerically greater than that of Jews, there was a far higher proportion of Jews in sales in relation to their total number in executive capacity.

Finally, the League heard some Jews and Christians give a stereotype of the Jew in the life insurance industry. These people expressed their belief that, by and large, Jews were disinterested in slow-moving administrative positions and preferred to remain in the selling end of the operation where financial returns were quicker and larger. This myth has almost become insurance industry folklore and is thoroughly exploded when one considers the substantial number of Jews who have willingly and deliberately chosen the relative security of such comparatively low-paid fields as government, teaching, and social work.

Furthermore, when pressed for particulars, those who expressed belief in the myth were able to point to few instances in which administrative openings were offered to Jews in the industry. When these instances were examined, it was acknowledged that the offers had been made to men who could accept them only at considerable financial sacrifice. Conversely, when these administrative jobs were offered to non-Jews, acceptance meant considerable financial advancement. In short, the more attractive administrative jobs were hardly ever offered to Jews in lesser-paying positions.

Another ADL study, pointing to an "under-utilization" of Jewish personnel, was made of eight of the largest commercial banks of the City of New York. This study encompassed the top officers and members of the boards of directors of these banks which are among the commercial giants of the American economy. It should be borne in mind that these banks are headquartered in a city with a Jewish population of well over two million, many of whom have achieved national recognition and prominence in all walks of life, including banking.

The eight banks studied had a total roster of 844 officers of the rank of vice president and above. Of this number, only thirty were of the Jewish faith. Of the thirty, twenty-two were found in two banks and seven in a third. Four banks had not a single Jew and the remaining bank had one.

With respect to boards of directors, the study showed that the eight banks had a total of 197 directors of whom three were of the Jewish faith, two in one bank and one in a second. Not unnaturally, these three were found in the two banks each of which had eleven Jewish officers.

These findings suggest an exclusionary pattern enforced

over the years notwithstanding all of the other social and economic factors in the City of New York that would seem to militate against such a practice.

Other than in such studies as the Insurance and the Banking surveys, statistical evidence is limited to cities such as Chicago and Los Angeles, where local human-relations agencies maintain records and conduct special surveys from time to time. Government agencies, trade unions, and many employers do not record religious affiliations. In addition, religious groups such as the Jews, unlike racial groups such as the Negroes, are not readily and visibly identifiable. (Of course, an employer who wishes to can usually determine without difficulty whether an applicant is Jewish.) Nevertheless, the data remain sketchy.

American Jews are sensitive to infringement on their occupational opportunities. They are aware of the many centuries when such deprivations were associated with second-class citizenship. They know, too, that America boasts of being different and *should be* different.

It must be clearly understood that the mass of Jewish immigrants came to this country from eastern Europe principally because the countries of their origin forbade them to engage in certain occupations, to reside in certain parts of the country, and to attend certain schools. They chose America because it was the land of opportunity. Although all the immigrants did not naively believe that the streets of the New World were literally paved with gold, they were hopeful that they would be free to work and support their families in human dignity. They did not mind the sweatshops, for they could see a future in which their children would work where they wished. The subsequent curtailment of their children's free choice of employment and industry is a betrayal of the dream America offered the immigrants, as well as a threat to the status of the immigrants' children.

Until the middle of the nineteenth century, America was truly the land of free economic opportunity it had appeared to be from across the ocean, even though the earliest settlers in colonial times transplanted remnants of Old World practices to the New World. For example, in 1655, the New Amsterdam Council affirmed restrictions on the freedom of Jews to engage in trade and to own real estate. But these restrictions were soon removed as vestigial remains of a feudal system which the consciously new society was eager to repudiate.

This is not to say that there were no differences in occupation among different ethnic groups. These differences involved background, habits, education, inherited capital, and family connections that were reflected in differences in occupation and industry. But there was no discrimination in employment *in principle* against a group such as the Jews. The right to "life, liberty and the pursuit of happiness" was a *public* guarantee implying, within its broad terms, a guarantee of the right to free employment—without which the general right was meaningless.

It was not until after the Civil War that a different principle concerning human rights began to be implicit: employment, as well as social relations, came to be thought of as a *private* affair, subject to limitations that private individuals could impose. By 1910, America was no longer the land of unlimited frontiers; there were fewer opportunities, and men competed more strenuously for them. The national wealth assumed a private, rather than public, color. And discrimination against Jews increased. Since the Jews were a group with many of the signs of their foreignness still upon them, the older settlers with a sense of pious justification could comfortably band against these people who since antiquity had been considered aliens. Social status, which was then being revived to bolster the claims of the old-timers to superiority, could most easily be invoked against the Jews, then conspicuously crowded in large numbers in the poorer sections of the big cities.

The links identified in previous pages now begin to form a chain: Jews could not afford to live in good neighborhoods so they herded together in slum areas; not knowing the language or customs of the new country, they stayed close to their co-religionists and did not associate with the other, longer-established groups; they worked in factories or as small businessmen on the periphery of trade. All these facts were adduced to explain why Jews as a group were undesirable—as residents of good neighborhoods, as friends, as employees in professional, managerial, or even in clerical positions.

CHAPTER 14.   **Doctor, Lawyer—or Indian Chief**

●

VETERINARIAN WANTED: Man or woman as assistant in small-animal practice in Michigan. State religious denomination, draft status, age, health, salary expected, and full particulars in first reply. . . .

Recent, gentile graduate wanted to join staff of southern California animal hospital. Much opportunity for case treatment and assisting in large surgical practice. Salary and apartment. A possibility of permanent arrangements dependent on ability of applicant. . . .

WANTED—assistant veterinarian in mixed practice in central Maryland. Salary—to be raised if satisfactory. Must be Christian. Car furnished. . . .

> —From the classified advertisements
> section of *The North American
> Veterinarian* magazine, early 1950s

The New York State Commission Against Discrimination has advised the Anti-Defamation League that the management of The North American Veterinarian has given "complete assurance that no advertising of a discriminatory nature will ever again appear in that publication." As a result, ADL's complaint against American Veterinary Publications reached a successful outcome through conciliation.

—From *Rights,* an ADL publication,
October 1956

Portola—Plumas County: Wanted young California licensed M.D. to assist two G.P.s during this summer and possibility of permanent association. Prefer Protestant or Catholic with two-year rotating internship. Portola (2200) is situated in the heart of the Feather River Country with exceptional recreational facilities such as fishing, hunting, golf. Very good schools. Salary open to discussion. . . .

Etna—Siskiyou County: Locum Tenens desired for the period of May 15th to August 15th, allowing about 1 week at the beginning before [the doctor] leaves for Europe. Large active general practice in well equipped office and clinic building; hospital facilities available 30 miles away in Yreka. Gentile preferred, California license necessary, personal interview required. . . .

—From California Medical Association
placement bulletin

We have never intended in any way to discriminate or to be a party to it through inadvertent repetition of statements furnished to us. In our efforts to provide a service to physicians, we have inadvertently misinterpreted the types of information regarding an opportunity that are desirable or useful. We are planning to re-evaluate our efforts in placement activities as well as our methods of serving as a source of information. I can assure you that we will screen the opportunity descriptions more closely and all references to race, color or creed will be deleted.

—Excerpt from a letter to a California
doctor from the California Medical
Association

The employment situation first became critical for American Jews in the professions in which traditionally they had played a large role; areas that were very attractive to second-generation American Jews whose parents had immigrated from eastern Europe. In ancient and early medieval times—and in modern times, whenever possible—Jews had been active as scholar "doctors." Study of ancient Jewish Law developed familiarity with medical, mathematical, physical, and legal concepts as they were used in religious lore. Since late in the Middle Ages, Jews in Europe had been barred from their ancient callings, but here in the New World they could return to their-first loves. Medicine, law, education, engineering—all these fields seemed open to persons of talent and offered a way of moving upward in the social scale that depended less on "connections" than on intelligence and education.

Unfortunately, around the turn of this century, there was a new development in American life that deterred those second-generation Jews who were eager to enter the professions. They came face to face with the consolidation of a kind of Establishment of professionals, somewhat resembling the British Establishment, which viewed its political, religious, and social functions as the preservation of power in the proper hands. To an extent the new American Establishment was a monopolistic response by the old-line professional leaders to the threat of competition from the children of the new immigrants, particularly those of the Jewish group. But as in all economic situations, a social component was inextricable from the purely material considerations. In this case, there was one factor as important as professional envy or malice—an unwillingness on the part of the established group to risk a loss of status that association with Jews in professional work might entail. There was already a pattern of social exclusion to justify employment discrimination in the high-social-status professions.

It was not easy at first to establish discrimination in depth against Jews in the professions: access to these fields was controlled by official regulation of educational requirements, apprenticeship, state licensing, membership in professional societies. Of the various professions, it was particularly difficult for the Law—with its quasipublic character, consisting of its association with courts, government organs, and the general "public interest"—to introduce discrimination against Jews. The legal Establishment had to content itself with placing obstacles in the way of Jewish employment in the "best" firms, which it did on the basis of social inferiority. Thus, indirectly, the ground was prepared for later restrictions on Jews at the source of their professional career—the law schools. By identifying Jewish lawyers with "inferior" companies and thus with a less elegant practice, the Establishment was able to project an image of the Jewish lawyer as intrinsically undesirable, in some genetic way a shady, underhanded character. Thus, students who might well develop into "shyster lawyers" were considered undesirable as applicants for law schools.

The educational profession, however, was able to be more "selective" at an earlier point—at the moment large numbers of Jews presented themselves as candidates for teaching positions. This was particularly true in the prestige institutions, slightly less so in other colleges and universities. In general, positions in institutions of higher education were regarded as naturally falling within the bailiwick of "native" Americans. In disseminating and interpreting Western culture, the descendants of immigrants from western Europe were "obviously" superior to Jews with their East-European and Mediterranean antecedents. Besides, the standards governing college and university appointments were responsive to the local prejudices of trustees. From 1870 to 1930, only a relatively few Jews found teaching positions in institutions of higher learning.

In public-school teaching, the situation was somewhat different. In this area, Jews had to compete not so much with long-established groups as with the sons and daughters of immigrants who had preceded them to American shores by no more than a generation or two. But in the larger cities, where these new ethnic groups resided, the municipal boards of education were often part of a city political machine in which Jews exerted no or only little influence. (This was so usually from choice, for the new Jewish immigrants brought with them an aversion to public authority inasmuch as their experience in the Old Country had been most unfortunate.) Therefore it was not until the civil-service system was adopted that Jewish teachers gradually joined the ranks of Irish teachers in such cities as New York. In other cities, not until after World War I were Jews able to teach freely in the public-school system—and then only because of the shortage of teachers as older ethnic-group members moved up to better-paying professional jobs.

The most serious form of exclusion developed in the medical profession—specifically in the medical societies and hospitals, which refused to admit qualified Jewish doctors. Here the connection between social discrimination and employment discrimination became most apparent. The medical societies were generally private associations; membership in them was often essential to establishing a successful practice since new physicians had to depend a great deal on referral from favorably disposed colleagues with established practices.

By the end of the first decade of the twentieth century, virtually all medical schools had devised quota systems to keep to a minimum the number of their Jewish students. It was felt by the policy-makers that these quotas were necessary because of the growing interest in the medical profession of the children of East-European Jewish immigrants. There is statistical evidence of the large attendance of Jews in colleges as early as 1908, and of their particularly strong interest in studying law and pharmacy. Medicine and dentistry were too expensive to attract large numbers of Jewish students. Their parents were just emerging from factories and small-business occupations. Ten years later the situation was quite different. In 1918–19, law was still very popular among Jewish students, but dentistry and medicine were gaining rapidly in popularity. By the early 1930s, about one eighth of the entering classes in American medical schools were Jewish. It was only the introduction of a subtle and extensive discriminatory system in most medical schools that subsequently reduced this percentage in the late thirties.

Despite the barriers raised by the quota systems, the great interest of Jewish students in law, medicine, and dentistry resulted in the middle thirties in the remarkably large number of Jews in these professions in communities throughout the United States. Thus, in San Francisco, eighteen of every thousand employed Jews were lawyers or judges, sixteen were doctors—compared to the city population as a whole, where five of every thousand were in the legal profession and five in the medical. There were similar ratios for Pittsburgh and Trenton.[83]

The exclusion of Jews from the "good" medical schools did affect their economic success adversely. During this period, Jewish physicians earned somewhat less than their non-Jewish colleagues, partly attributable to the lower ranking of the medical schools where they had studied.

The increase in the number of Jewish professionals has continued, although not in medicine. Jews have moved into other accessible professions. There is now an increasing number of Jewish journalists, authors, engineers, architects, and college teachers. In the two decades since the highly discriminatory thirties, there has been a rapid rise in the number of Jews engaged in *all* intellectual occupations.

An interesting example of this diversion in Jewish professionalization during the past quarter-century is afforded by Charleston, South Carolina.[84] In the middle thirties, the Jews of that city—long-established, with a relatively low proportion of immigrants—included one doctor, one dentist, several lawyers, two pharmacists, three or four teachers, and one rabbi. By 1948, in the wake of the shift of professional interest, there were eight doctors, seven dentists, eighteen lawyers, five pharmacists, nine teachers, and four rabbis. There were also eighteen engineers, seven social workers, four accountants, three radio commentators, three writers and editors, three artists, and an orchestra leader. Yet the Jewish community numbered fewer than two thousand.

A contributing factor in the spread of the Jewish professional group has been the upgrading of the status of skilled workers both in business and in the communications industry. A generation ago a business technician such as the accountant, or a mass-media specialist such as a radio broadcaster would not have been regarded as a professional having virtually equal status with a physician. This is part of a general trend toward the upgrading of all consumer services which, in turn, is related to the growth in the importance of these services in the national economy.

The history of Jewish white-collar employment and professional employment is similar in many respects. Discrimination against Jewish white-collar workers also grew steadily during the early 1900s. The restrictions were relaxed somewhat because of the manpower shortage of World War I, as they were again to be relaxed during World War II. During the twenties there was a revival and intensification of this white-collar discrimination. By the time of the Great Depression of the thirties, discrimination against Jews had become characteristic of many of the nation's largest enterprises. It was justified on the ground that personnel policies—even prejudicial ones—were purely a private concern, even though some of these enterprises were chartered by the state or were public utilities.

Even so, during this same decade many children of Jewish immigrants became clerks, secretaries, salesmen, and other kinds of white-collar worker. This has been verified in almost every study of Jewish communities. In Buffalo (1938), Detroit (1935), and San Francisco (1938), the "clerks and kindred" category constituted the largest group in the Jewish working population. Broken down by industry, the greatest number were in trade. But a large part of those classified as engaged in "trade" were neither proprietors nor managers; they were clerks or salespeople.

(Interestingly enough, it was the Jewish women who were most concentrated in white-collar work, at a period when working women were still somewhat of a novelty. One study conducted in 1933 showed 51 per cent of the gainfully employed Jewish women of New York engaged in clerical and sales positions, compared with 29 per cent of the working women in the general city population. In other cities, the concentration of women workers was even greater: Buffalo had 78 per cent of the Jewish working women in white-collar work in 1938, Detroit 66 per cent in 1935, Passaic 63 per cent in 1937.)[85]

What is the explanation for this apparent paradox: a rise in the number and proportion of Jewish white-collar workers during the thirties, the same decade in which the rise in discrimination occurred?

This is explainable in part by the Jewish group's traditional drive toward an independent economic position. History taught the Jews to adopt a defensive stance in the face of religious and economic discrimination; this practice served them well during a period of emergency such as the depression. Jews selected three employment methods to combat economic difficulties caused by discrimination. The first was self-employment; the second was the development of economic pursuits within the Jewish orbit. (The independent operator of a business, or the professional man, could at any time move on with his capital and his skill. This was better than being dependent on hostile non-Jews for a job. By working for and with fellow Jews he was more fully assured of some support, however minimal.) Third, Jews took shelter under the wings of those occupations that were immune from discriminatory infection because of their public character. This was possible in a democratic society where the government was not hostile to any group but protected its right to work in occupations with a "public interest."

Hence, even at the low point of the national economy during the depression years, the Jewish working force may have suffered less than other groups.

Studies of Jewish communities during the thirties showed Jews exhibiting their famous "strength in adversity." By making a virtue of economic necessity—or practicing the virtue learned by their parents—they remained somewhat protected in the generally stricken communities. True, Jewish clerks and salespeople generally earned less than their non-Jewish counterparts, although white-collar workers as a group suffered less than other workers. And, as previously noted, proportionately more Jews than non-Jews were employed at such labor. The heavier Jewish employment in white-collar work was due, at least in part, to the proportionately larger number of Jews who were engaged in trade as proprietors of their own businesses, and who themselves did not discriminate *against* fellow Jews in employing help. This enabled the Jewish working force as a whole to avoid the anti-Jewish prejudice of many of the large private corporations. (In 1937, only one eighth as many Jews as non-Jews, proportionately, were working in public utilities in New York City.) The defensive avoidance of potentially discriminatory situations extended during this period to business bureaucracies in general, for the practical reason that there was normally less opportunity in such places for personal advancement on the basis of talent, the premium being on social contacts.

In group behavior, as in all human relations, attitudes that arise in response to extreme situations are slow to disappear even though the critical stresses seem to be relieved. The discrimination of the thirties has relaxed greatly, but the Jewish group as a whole continues to exercise the tried-and-true formula for escape from potential discrimination. Thus, in the sixties, each of the two large occupational groups of American Jews most directly affected by economic discrimination in the recent past has retained a typical way of skirting the possibility again of facing that discrimination. The white-collar workers—principally women—have restricted themselves to jobs in nondiscriminatory, often Jewish-owned, industries; and the professionals often divert their ambitions to professions that are their second or third choice. A typical example is the Jew who is fearful of not being admitted to a medical school and therefore applies to a dental school.

The obvious resulting imbalance has had a deteriorating effect not on the economic status of the American Jew but on his social and psychological acceptance. Sociologists point out that an economic function can become either a means of alienation or one of integration. A businessman who finds it advisable to do business among his co-religionists is more comfortable with persons whose habits and manners he knows, and to whose needs he may cater more successfully than can an outsider. But at the same time, he is missing the contact with other groups and the opportunity to observe other mores. He is under no compulsion to conform with their code of behavior—and inevitably serious misunderstandings between himself and "the others" develop during their casual meetings.

These misunderstandings—and the accompanying feeling of uneasiness on the part of both parties—supply the general ground-tone out of which rise specific forms of discrimination. With the growing acculturation of the Jewish group in the United States and a parallel easing of strain in relations between the Jewish groups and other groups, discrimination has been on the wane since the end of World War II. But enough of it remains to call first for documentation and then for a description of the deliberate efforts of interested parties in mitigating, if not eradicating, anti-Jewish discrimination in employment in the United States.

CHAPTER 15.   **The White-Collar Worker**

●

In June 1959, Otto Preisler, President of the Home Federal Savings and Loan Association, sent the following letter to 23 Chicago employment agencies.

Gentlemen:

There seems to be some misunderstanding among a few of the employment agencies servicing our account with respect to our employment policy. For many years our employment policy has been based on merit regardless of race, creed, color or national origin.

Please, therefore, when referring applicants to us in the future, make such referral solely on the basis of the individual's experience and qualifications for the particular vacancy available.

We will appreciate it if you would bring this letter to the attention of the placement representatives in your agency who service our employment orders.

Very truly yours,

"For many years our employment has been based on merit . . ."—or so Mr. Preisler sincerely thought. Until, that is, a spokesman for the Anti-Defamation League cautioned him against believing that it was just the solitary error of a personnel director that led his bank to discriminate against a young Jewish girl.

Mr. Preisler had told an old friend, a prominent Jewish builder in the mid-West, that he had hit the ceiling when he first learned that his bank was suspected by the League of turning away a job applicant because of her religion. The charge couldn't possibly have any basis in fact, he argued. Why, he had never even laid down any special hiring rules, much less restrictions against Jews. His anger was directed at his own people, not at the League for bringing it to his attention. How could his bank have created such a false impression?

Earlier that year, on February 6, 1959, an attractive young lady had completed her studies at the local International Business Machines training center in Chicago and was interviewed by the school's placement counsellor. Satisfied that she was equipped to handle a skilled job in her chosen field, the counsellor telephoned the Home Federal Savings about her.

Yes, they could use a competent IBM operator in the Auditing Department. Wouldn't the counsellor please send the girl over for an interview the next day. By the way, what was her name?

"Vivian Edelstein."

There was a pause at the other end. "Is she Jewish?"

The placement counsellor ignored the irrelevant question, simply asking instead what time they wanted the girl to be there.

"Any time in the morning."

Vivian arrived right after nine, was taken to an IBM machine where she showed her proficiency. She was then led to the desk of a vice-president in Audit. After a short talk the executive said he was quite satisfied with her, adding that he really didn't need a girl with tremendous experience. This was a new function for the bank, he explained, and they both could learn as they went along. He asked her what church she attended.

"I don't go to a church. I go to a synagogue."

"I thought so from your name," he said unhappily. "I have never had a Jewish girl before. Usually when someone with a name like yours applies for a job, they put her off for one reason or another until they can find somebody else. It's the policy of the firm not to hire Jews—but fill out the application form and I will see."

When Vivian returned home she received a message from Mr. Veenstra, the Vice-President, saying that he needed a girl with more experience. But her mother, a working woman, was angry and unwilling to let the matter rest. The next day she told her own employer the whole story. He, in turn, became so incensed that he immediately telephoned Mr. Veenstra and castigated the bank for its act of prejudice.

Minutes later he received a return call from Home Federal's personnel director who wanted him to know that the bank was not guilty. The girl had clearly misunderstood. The bank did not, insisted the man from Personnel, practice religious discrimination in its employment policy.

That night Vivian received two phone calls. The first was from the personnel director urging her to return the next day for another interview. The second call was from the man who had interviewed her, Mr. Veenstra, the Vice-President, who wanted her to know how sorry he was about the whole thing and that he hoped that he would see her in the morning. However, Vivian's mother refused to permit her to re-apply for the job, insisting that she inform the bank of her lack of interest and then report the whole affair to the Anti-Defamation League.

Hearing the details of the story, the League caseworker

could not conclude that there was real evidence of culpability; certainly the bank officials had gone out of their way after working hours, to urge Vivian to come in again. Routinely, however, an ADL inquiry was made at the office of the Chicago Bureau on Jewish Employment Problems, a human-relations agency concerned solely with the problems of employment discrimination.

The Bureau's records showed that in the period from June 1953 to February 1958, five employment agencies in Chicago had reported 21 discriminatory job orders placed by the Home Federal Savings and Loan Association. The last eight discriminatory orders had been placed by the bank's personnel director. One of the agencies quoted him as saying that "Jews are not wanted and are never to be referred."

At the first meeting with Mr. Preisler, it became clear to League representatives that he was guilty of nothing more than a lack of awareness of discriminatory practices. He argued vehemently that the Home Federal had no such policy. The discussion, however, made it evident that the bank had no rules either way; in the absence of an affirmatively-stated merit policy, lesser executives in the bank apparently had taken it upon themselves to initiate a policy that barred Jews.

Mr. Preisler obviously had never before given the matter serious consideration. Now that he thought about it he could remember five or six Jews on the bank's staff. True, only two of them had sought time off to observe the Jewish holidays the year before; the others, he believed, had not asked leave because they did not wish to draw attention to the fact that they were Jewish.

In any case, Mr. Preisler now viewed the situation seriously. At the end of the conferences with the League, he decided upon a series of five steps that would protect the bank from ever again falling into the trap of discrimination. One of these steps was his letter to the 23 employment agencies operating in the Chicago metropolitan area.

Toward the end of 1956, the Bureau on Jewish Employment Problems of Chicago published a summary of its findings on employment practices of major business firms in that city. The examination had revealed that of 20,000 job orders placed with Chicago commercial employment agencies in a six month period of that year, about 18 per cent barred Jews from consideration.

In that same period the Anti-Defamation League, together with the Bureau, also studied the experiences of 5600 applicants at a Chicago employment agency, and developed equally disturbing findings. This study showed that 20 out of every 100 Protestant applicants, and 17 out of every 100 Catholic applicants, were placed in jobs by the agency, whereas only 9 out of every 100 Jewish applicants could be placed.

The nature of these findings was not unexpected; in a random sample four years earlier, licensed employment counselors said they had found Jews to be the hardest of the three major religious groups to place in jobs. None of the counselors found that Protestants or Catholics fell within the categories they used to describe Jewish job applicants: *hard to place* and *never placed, even if qualified*—but 46 per cent of the counselors polled, after saying Protestants were easiest to place, put Jews in these difficult categories.

Apparently, the more serious discrimination practiced against Negroes does not serve as a lightning rod to attract discriminatory electricity away from Jewish homes or as a magnet to pick up all the charged particles of prejudice in the area. Rather, where a broad sentiment of prejudice is expressed in discriminatory practices, Jews seem also to be affected unfavorably by the prevalent climate of opinion.

In the Chicago area a large-scale, over-all pattern of discrimination prevails in housing, education, and social intercourse. It would be an error to single out employment agencies as the villains. They are simply responding to the area's mores. Chicago's industrial complex must be assigned prime responsibility for economic discrimination. If anything, employment agencies are as much the victims of the discriminatory practices as they are perpetrators.

The executive editor of the Chicago Bureau on Jewish Employment Problems commented in this manner on the commercial agency's attitude toward discrimination:

There is among the agency heads and the individual employment counselors the usual incidence of racial and religious prejudices. Their tendencies to initiate discrimination are curbed, however, by the profit motive in the business. Even the most discriminatory of these will, therefore, try to place Jewish applicants, if necessary by special solicitation, when their file of current orders have barriers against Jewish employees. Moreover, they are constantly facing discriminatory choices of employers, not only as regards Negroes, Jews and other minority groups, but as to Catholics, Protestants and a wide variety of nationality groups; so it is the unusual counselor or agency head who is not personally rubbed the wrong way by the discrimination exercised by employers. They generally, therefore, would prefer an end to the problem of discrimination since it would provide them with a much more straightforward and profitable operation. A number of employment agency heads in Chicago have indicated, for instance, their private support of an FEP bill, believing this would strengthen their own hand in dealing with the discriminatory limitations employers impose upon them.[86]

Throughout the fifties, there was a desperate shortage of qualified clerical workers; some firms spent months trying to fill vacancies. Gradually, they relaxed the rigid requirements for these jobs, finally retaining only one—a qualification based exclusively on prejudice: *No Jews*. The criteria adopted during the depression had persisted into a prosperity period; Chicago Jews were forced to turn to their own group for white-collar work opportunities.

The Chicago studies also showed that at least 20 per cent of the applicants were Jews, although only an estimated 8 per cent of the entire city population is Jewish. These figures throw light on the accuracy of a persistent miscomprehension as to the character of Jewish employment and industry in the United States. As previously noted, there is a relatively large proportion of Jews who are content with moderate-paying white-collar jobs. The mere fact that many Jews continue to apply for white-collar jobs in so discriminatory an area as Chicago is convincing proof of the basic Jewish willingness to accept security at a lower level.

The list of industries that discriminate against Jews is a good index to the area of Jewish economic activity in this country. This data confirms the widely discussed study conducted in 1936 by *Fortune* Magazine. There has been no apparent significant change in Jewish industrial strength since then; Jews are still weak in certain key industries that continue to practice discrimination. The *Fortune* article noted:

On the New York Stock Exchange, 252 of the 1375 members, or 18 per cent are Jews, while 55 of the 637 firms listed by the Exchange directory are Jewish, 24 are half-Jewish, and 39 have dominant Jewish influence.

The absence of Jews in the insurance business is noteworthy. In the insurance agency field, however, about half the business is Jewish in New York. And the New York insurance brokerage business is predominantly Jewish, although the three or four nationwide brokerage houses with New York offices are non-Jewish. Outside New York, Jewish representation follows the Jewish population pattern.

If the Jews have a subordinate place in finance, which they

are often said to control, they have an even more inconspicuous place in heavy industry. The only outstanding Jews in that field are the Blocks, largely interested in Inland Steel, and Mr. Max Epstein, Chairman of the Board of General American Transportation Corporation, which manufactures tank cars. Inland Steel is a successful company, well liked and much respected in the trade, but its share of the steel business is relatively small. The only exception to the rule that steel is not a Jewish industry is the scrap business. Scrap iron and steel is owned 90 per cent, being an outgrowth of the junk business, which at the end of the last century was in the hands of Russian Jews. It may be added in passing that practically the whole waste products industry including nonferrous scrap metal (a $300,000,000 a year business in 1929), paper, cotton, rag, wool rag, and rubber, is Jewish. . . . But the clothing business is the spectacular and outstanding exception to the statement that Jewish industrial interests are generally in the minority. Not even in the liquor business, which was always the prerogative of the Jew in Poland, not in the tobacco business, in which many a rich Jew made his start, are Jewish interests dominant. . . .

It becomes apparent that Jews are most frequently to be found in those reaches of industry where manufacturer and merchant meet. Consequently their predominance in retailing might be expected. It will not be found. . . .

The department store chains like May, Allied, Interstate, and Gimbel are Jewish, but the Five and Ten, etc., chains like Woolworth and Kress are 95 per cent not. In the food and grocery field, where the greatest numbers of chains operate, 95 to 99 per cent, including A & P, are non-Jewish. Montgomery Ward in the mail-order field is non-Jewish, while Sears, Roebuck has a Jewish history (Julius Rosenwald), but active management of Sears, Roebuck now is in the hands of General Robert Wood. Drug store chains are about 90 per cent non-Jewish and apparel store chains 90 per cent the other way. Jews are in a definite retailing minority over the country.[87]

The 1956 Chicago figures, which corroborate *Fortune*'s findings of a quarter of a century earlier, are in turn confirmed by data from two other areas—Ohio and California. The Ohio Governor's Advisory Commission on Civil Rights published a report in December 1958, after an extensive state-wide survey. As in Chicago, it reported a pattern of discrimination against Jews in certain industries and services—in banks, utilities, and manufacturing companies, especially those engaged in heavy industry. It is significant to note that these are the very parts of the economy that the *Fortune* article described as definitely not under Jewish influence. The close connection between the trades where Jews work and those which they own is apparent.

In Ohio, too, the nonwhites were described as suffering far more seriously than Jews from prejudice in employment possibilities. Yet, in community after community, Jewish leaders have emphasized the deleterious effect on the self-respect of the local Jewish community caused by the anti-Jewish discrimination that did exist.

In California, during the latter part of 1958 and the early months of 1959, employment discrimination against Jews (again in the context of a general pattern directed mostly against nonwhites) was particularly high in the Los Angeles area. Here, discriminating firms included insurance companies, banks, department stores, oil companies, transportation lines, real estate agencies, food processors, and manufacturers of many different products—a cross section of the local industry.

These studies of discrimination do not say that Jewish white-collar workers who eventually did find employment in unprejudiced firms suffered irredeemable financial loss. In Los Angeles, as elsewhere in the country, Jewish white-collar workers, once employed, were comparatively well paid. A percentage distribution of the annual income of the heads of households in the Jewish population of Los Angeles at this time with respect to clerical and sales jobs was: 33.4 per cent earn less than $4000; 49.9 per cent earn between $4000 and $8000; 16.7 per cent earn over $8000. During this period, the average national income for each family was about $6000. The cost of living in the Los Angeles area was relatively high, and the average large-city income is probably higher than the national average. On the basis of these figures, some half of the Los Angeles Jewish white-collar families had incomes above the national average.

Despite the high incidence of biased requests for white-collar workers that prospective employers address to employment agencies in these three areas (Chicago, Ohio, and Los Angeles) it would be a mistake to regard the situation as deteriorating in the country as a whole. Nevertheless, studies in other areas yield somewhat similar results. For example:

San Francisco

In 1956, the Institute of Industrial Relations of the University of California surveyed employment discrimination against Jews in the San Francisco Bay area and reported that of 340 private employers in major industries interviewed, 75 employers, or 22 per cent, acknowledged that they followed a policy of discriminating against Jews. They either barred Jews completely or listed their employment on a quota basis. This figure may run higher, as not all firms interviewed replied fully to all questions.

Denver

An ADL survey in Denver, Colorado, in 1956, found that 45 out of 46 public and private employment agencies had agreed to service a request for a "white Protestant" secretary.[88]

In short, there is serious reason for accepting the premise that in the white-collar echelon of American big business all is not what it should be in a democratic society.

CHAPTER 16.   **Change for the Better**

●

. . . I am hopeful and confident that from this time forward the committee will exercise the great powers given to it by Executive order to permanently remove, from Government employment and work performed for the Government, every trace of discrimination because of race, creed, color or place of national origin.

The Executive order creating this committee and granting to it powerful sanctions is both an announcement of our determination to end job discrimination once and for all and an effective instrument to realize that objective.

. . . the distinguished public officials and private citizens who make up the committee, carry the responsibility for implementing equal employment policies in Government and work under Government contracts.

This responsibility I know will be discharged with fairness, with understanding, with an open mind and a generous spirit of cooperation—and also with firmness. There is no intention to make this a harsh or unreasonable mandate for those sincerely and honestly seeking compliance, nor is there any intention to compromise the principle of equality in employment. American citizens unjustly denied the opportunity to work for the Government, for those doing business with the Government, will have that opportunity.

. . . The Federal Government spends billions of dollars a year and therefore this is a most powerful instrument for accomplishing the objective which we all seek. All of us agree that Federal money should not be spent in any way which encourages discrimination, but rather should be spent in such a way that it encourages the national goal of equal opportunity. And when Federal budgets are as large as they are, when they cover such a large percentage of employed people of this country, directly or indirectly, this quite obviously can be a very effective instrument to carry out the national objective. . . .

> —President John F. Kennedy at a
> meeting in the White House on
> April 11, 1961, of the President's
> Committee on Equal Employment
> Opportunity

On the whole, there is much less willingness in the United States today to accept racial and religious employment discrimination as natural or as the private privilege of business than there has been in the past. Even among those who have themselves been guilty of discriminatory practices, one finds sincere receptivity to the idea of Fair Employment Practices legislation. During the past twenty-five years, employment agencies testify, there has been a vast improvement in the situation. In the late thirties, the agencies estimate, as high as 95 per cent of their job orders were pegged as closed to Jews. As a result, some of these agencies posted signs in their offices announcing *Jews need not apply,* while others refused even to register Jews, turning them away at the reception desk. Still others maintained separate files for Jewish applicants for the benefit of those occasional employers who ventured to hire them. Current studies revealing that about 25 per cent of job orders are marked *No Jews* means a decrease of 70 per cent in discriminatory job orders.

This significant decrease must be closely related to the clear shift in employer sentiment. Employers are now expressing more and more a policy of no religious or racial preferences. This definite shift in employer attitude made it possible for the California Employment Agencies Association to adopt a resolution calling on member organizations to remove all potentially discriminatory questions from their employment forms, *and to refrain from soliciting restrictions when an employer did not voluntarily state his preferences* [our italics].

Even when an "employer" states a discriminatory preference, the company he represents may actually have no such prejudiced policy. One tends to assume that discriminatory employment practices always are dictated by the deliberate exclusionary directives of industry's leadership. That may originally have been the case, but many recent private conferences with the top management of "prejudiced" companies have bared a paradoxical, all-too-human situation: often personnel offices in large firms are practicing discrimination in hiring without the knowledge of—in fact, against the actual desires of—top management.

How is one to interpret this discrepancy between the democratic wishes of top management toward workers of all creeds and the bigoted practices of underlings against Jewish workers? It may be another illustration of the different rate at which attitudes change; executives who are more aware of the economic implications of discrimination (and perhaps of the social ones as well), are more quickly ready to abandon fixed ideas as to the desirability of certain groups of workers. Too, there is always the personal element: personnel workers, closer to the working force than top management, may be more responsive to an underlying dislike harbored by the veteran workers for Jews as fellow workers. This dislike can perhaps be traced to the conditioning of a no-Jewish-workers tradition in a particular company.

But whatever the background for the change in attitudes toward Jewish employment opportunities, there is today an undoubted difference, a clear improvement. "Help Wanted" advertisements, second in importance only to employment agencies as a method of screening out prospective Jewish applicants for white-collar positions, no longer blatantly state "Gentiles Only" or "Christians Preferred," the common practice during the thirties. Newspapers, often on their own, sometimes by stricture of a statewide civil-rights law, and sometimes under the pressure of a human-relations agency, no longer normally accept such advertising.

In larger terms, what the United States has witnessed since the depression, with its concurrent massive employment discrimination, has been a shift in public attitude parallel with (or perhaps ahead of) a shift in public consciousness—whose expression ultimately is the law. The first legal outlawing of employment discrimination came in connection with public service, where the public interest was apparent. Early measures had occasionally ruled out religious preference in civil-service appointments. Then, some four or five years after the depression, federal directives and state laws were enacted forbidding discriminatory practices on the part of employers or workers whose work was connected with the government—in New Jersey, in public works; in New York, in public utilities; in Wisconsin, in public schools. Presidential executive orders prohibited racial and religious discrimination by federal contractors or subcontractors. After 1940, an increasingly large part of American industry was tied to Washington as a result of the mounting volume of defense orders and was thus subject to such antidiscriminatory regulations. Beginning in 1942, efforts to enact Fair Employment Practices (FEP) laws on the federal level failed; successive bills could not surmount the hurdle of Southern filibusters in the Senate.

On the state level, New York and New Jersey took the first steps in 1945, and year by year the number of states and municipalities with FEP ordinances and commissions has grown. By September 1961, twenty-one states, including recently California, Ohio, Illinois, and Missouri, had enacted enforceable FEP laws covering a total population of over 70 million. One other state, Indiana, had passed FEP legislation without enforcement provisions. In addition, some forty cities had passed ordinances against employment discrimination, some of them carrying provisions for enforcement.

The FEP laws are not a cure-all, especially for Jews. Enforcement is difficult, evasion by subterfuge easy. The most subtle subterfuge occurs in employment of Jews and the continuance of barriers to advancement *after* hiring. But the laws have proved important for their educational role and have helped to create a public standard of what is legal and just. Since most people prefer to act legally and justly—sometimes even when deep and conflicting emotions are involved —the FEP laws have helped to call into question old, unthinking practices based on prejudice. Of the various forms of religious discrimination, employment is proving to be the least deep-rooted and, as a consequence, Jews are finding increasing employment in clerical occupations that not so long ago were barred to them.

Other occupations, in which social status remains important, present a more formidable challenge. The findings established by the Anti-Defamation League in its studies in the banking, insurance and automobile industries indicates that by and large, the executive level in many strategically important industries are still closed and the professions with "prestige"—medicine and law—continue to discriminate against Jewish students and practitioners. Vast changes in social discrimination will have to occur before meaningful progress can be made in the higher executive areas of big business.

What is the meaning of the term *discrimination* in the context of the relatively large number of Jews who have succeeded in professional careers despite social barriers? When a member of a "minority" group (a Jew) and a member of a "majority" group (a white non-Jew) have the same or similar personality qualifications and academic records but do not have an equal opportunity to compete for the same professional job, discrimination is taking place. This is true—even if the Jew may have a very good opportunity to obtain some other job, perhaps a highly attractive one. The Jewish applicant is the victim of discrimination if his opportunities for available jobs are limited solely because of his religious identification.

With this definition in mind, one must conclude from the evidence obtained from a number of reputable sources that Jewish professionals *are* the targets of discrimination in job placement.

At institutions of higher learning, placement officers refer students trained at their schools to openings in their fields of competence. Their reports are conclusive: Two out of three law professors in a position to know the facts state that they can place almost any student, *but the chances that a Jew will get a top job are definitely poorer than those of a white Gentile.*[89]

Related data show that the same odds held some years ago against Jewish law-school graduates both in type of employment and in income.[90] In 1948, Jewish law-school graduates were given employment in private industry only a third as often as were non-Jewish graduates. And nearly twice the proportion of Jews as of non-Jews were in the lowest-paying classification, that of salaried law clerk. Half of all Jewish lawyers who were graduated in the years 1946 and 1947 and who were in full-time legal work earned fifteen dollars less per week than non-Jewish law graduates of the same years. Finally, regardless of classification, the Jewish lawyer, with few exceptions, earned about three hundred dollars less a year than the non-Jewish lawyer. It is hardly surprising, then, that wherever possible Jewish lawyers have shunned non-Jewish firms. In New York City, nine out of ten Jewish lawyers reported that they were associated with a firm in which some or all of the partners were Jewish. In other areas of the country, the ratio was about eight out of ten.

Engineering is a profession whose importance has grown tremendously since World War II. After teaching, it is now the largest of the professions. There has been an increasing interest among Jews in this field in the last few decades. A census of Jewish college students completed by the B'nai B'rith Vocational Service Bureau as long ago as October 1946 showed that nearly 17 per cent of the Jewish students enrolled in professional schools and departments at the time were studying engineering—a higher proportion than in any other professional field except business administration and education. Intensive efforts by the federal government in recent years to coax an increasing number of students into science and engineering so that the nation's booming scientific industry would not lack trained manpower has raised even higher the proportion of Jews moving into this field.

Engineering professors concerned with the placement of graduates have described four different discriminatory techniques used by employers who applied for help. The first technique is an absolute policy of hiring no Jews at all; this is rarely applied, but apparently there are some 100-per-cent non-Jewish companies. A second, more frequent, policy is to impose an informal over-all quota on Jews to be employed. The third policy, quite prevalent in many parts of the nation, is to restrict the hiring of Jews to certain kinds of jobs. The fourth form of discrimination is the requirement that the Jewish applicant be superior to the non-Jewish applicant for the same job. If a Jewish and a non-Jewish job candidate are approximately equal in training and background, the discriminatory company will invariably pick the non-Jew.

Unfortunately, these four techniques do not by any means exhaust the devices employed to bar qualified Jews from desirable professional jobs. The following extract from the 1952 files of the New York State Commission Against Discrimination is a concrete example of how employment agencies prevent Jewish candidates for professional jobs from being considered:

Job Specification Used as a Subterfuge:

A verified complaint against an employment agency charged that the respondent refused to refer complainant to a position as chemist because of his creed. The complainant alleged that the interviewer noted from the application that the complainant had graduated from City College of the City of New York with a Bachelor of Science degree, and inquired whether he had studied biology; that the complainant replied that he had studied biology and was thereupon rejected with statement that the employer had specifically requested a person with a B.S. degree who had not studied biology. Complainant alleged that he was qualified for the position in question, that inquiry with respect to the study of biology was a subterfuge, and that the complainant was in fact refused a referral because of his creed, which was indicated to the respondent by his name and his graduation from a college where a large percentage of the students is Jewish. Investigation established that the prospective employer disqualified only those applicants who have majored in biology, but that the study of biology in itself is not a disqualification provided the applicant had studied general, physical, organic, qualitative and quantitative chemistry. The complainant had studied the required subjects. The Investigating Commissioner found that the complainant's educational background was not so different from that of other applicants who were referred by the respondent to the prospective employer for the position of chemist as to warrant his preclusion from consideration by the employer. . . .[91]

Another profession with a noticeable rate of discrimination against Jews is accounting. The following is the result of a study of the fifteen largest public accounting firms in Cincinnati. Of the 286 accountants employed in these firms, only three were Jews, and one of these was a partner in one of the firms. Over a period of approximately thirty years, only fourteen Jews, including the three mentioned, had been employed in these accounting firms.[92]

What conclusions can be drawn from all this?

First, that Jews who wish to enter upon professional careers in the United States at the present time may expect to encounter obstacles before securing entry to a professional school, and—after the completion of an arduous course of study—from prospective employers, their agents, and clients. They will find this discrimination extending through most areas where professionals are employed. Their own university placement offices (who themselves sometimes accept discriminatory job orders) may well have trouble in placing them in the more desirable positions. They may be expected to be superior to their non-Jewish classmates. If they are selected for the job, they will have to accept smaller salaries offering less opportunity for advancement in non-Jewish firms or else retreat to the safety of Jewish-owned firms or a strictly Jewish clientele.

Does this sound hopeless? Actually, it is not. Discrimination is only an irritant for an American who is a Jew in the United States, not a crippling disability as it is for the American who is a Negro. The attitude of the public has become much more democratic during the past thirty years. The serious need for professional skills in our country will increase, not diminish. American business, industry, and labor leaders have openly agreed with Elmo Roper's assertion that the United States cannot afford the cost of discrimination, estimated at roughly thirty billion dollars per year.

Of all forms of discrimination, employment discrimination is the least virulent because non-Jews profess themselves more willing to work than to live alongside Jews or to associate with them on a personal-friendship basis. For this reason, in untangling the web of anti-Jewish discrimination in the United States, employment discrimination is probably the easiest target for attack. Since discrimination against Jews— or any other minority group—in any form is interdependent and interrelated with all other forms, the elimination of any single facet of this undemocratic phenomenon weakens all the others. And this is the goal of all decent-minded Americans.

V. "SOME OF MY
BEST FRIENDS . . ."

●

This has been a book about problems, not solutions. It is manifestly far easier to accumulate and report the facts in any given situation than it is to formulate an effective means of resolving the difficulties described. We did not write such a book because, first, we did not set out to write one of this nature, and second, because we have no panaceas to offer.

However, were we to attempt a presentation in depth of the solutions to religious-discriminatory practices, we would probably begin such a work (as we did this book) with the knottiest issue—social discrimination. This area of the over-all problem is the least susceptible to elimination or correction by law and legislation. Its practice contributes to a way of life that will not easily be changed by exhortation. It is part of a tradition of polite, snobbish prejudice now so deeply rooted in American society that it will not respond quickly to a formal educative process. It will take an intensive and extensive educational program at every level of community life to pry it loose from its moorings.

The area of housing, which is also quite fundamental to

the entire question of prejudicial customs in our nation, may be a better starting point for those forces interested in trying corrective measures.

Civil rights in the United States took a giant step forward between 1945 and the 1960s, probably the greatest single advance for any period since the Bill of Rights became the law of the land. The first ten amendments to the American Constitution wrought tremendous changes in a way of life that had been traditional to the former English colonists; now, once again, additional advances in the basic human rights of people have come about by means of the law.

In the present period, with its vastly more complicated political structure, each of the three great branches of the federal government contributed to the growing body of law designed to ensure or enlarge the legal guarantees of equal human rights. Beginning in the administration of Franklin Roosevelt, a series of executive orders was issued concerning civil rights that now range from the control of Navy personnel aboard an aircraft carrier to employment rules for corporations doing business with the Agriculture Department. In the same period, the Supreme Court has handed down innumerable civil-rights decisions, including decrees about Negro schoolchildren, the non-enforceability of restrictive covenants in deeds of real property, the rights of people to swim at public beaches, and so on. The federal legislature, too, has enacted laws designed to strengthen individual human rights in still other ways.

Law is an effective method for changing the mores of a nation, notwithstanding the accepted theory that statutes, decrees, and judicial decisions can control only overt acts of discrimination—not prejudicial attitudes. The fact is that when the actual behavior of an entire society is modified by law, more often than not the attitudes of that society eventually change to conform to the legal rules of conduct. This makes it, then, even more compelling that the law be used to correct the denial of equal rights to members of minority groups.

Although we asserted at the outset of this book and repeated our conviction that all religious discrimination is interdependent, linked together in an endless chain, we nevertheless believe that prejudice in housing provides as strong a link as social discrimination for all the other bias practices. This means that housing is an excellent starting point, if one is needed, for an attack by law on the whole structure of minority prejudice in America.

Not long ago a federal commission of inquiry asked the Anti-Defamation League, among others, for its views on the use of law to achieve equality of housing opportunity. In submitting its answer, the ADL suggested steps the federal government could and should take toward this goal. ADL's formal statement said in part:

The federal government has long recognized that it plays an important role in the task of insuring for every American family a decent place to live. It was to achieve this purpose that a number of laws were enacted by Congress providing for the erection of public housing built with federal aid and establishing several programs aimed at encouraging the creation of decent housing not only by local government but also by private industry.

The Federal Housing Administration is committed in principle to "equality of opportunity irrespective of race, color, creed or national origin." The housing agencies of the federal government have acknowledged that they, pursuant to the due process and equal protection provisions of the Federal Constitution, are bound to a national policy of nondiscrimination in the use and expenditure of federal funds.

The years that have elapsed since the historic U.S. Supreme Court decision in the public school cases have demonstrated that the federal government, in all its branches, must take every possible action to insure equal protection of the laws for all. It is duty bound under the Constitution to insure that federal funds and the federal credit are not used to strengthen and entrench practices of discrimination.

It follows from this that those responsible for the administration of the federal housing program must forthrightly declare their acceptance of the national policy of non-discrimination in carrying out their duties of administering the federal housing program. They must make it clear that they will not permit this program to be used either to impress new patterns of segregation on housing anywhere in our country or to strengthen or maintain such existing patterns.

Thus, the federal housing agencies should reorient their practices and their existing procedures to embody in them specific requirements that those seeking the aid of the federal government in connection with the production of housing must undertake a binding commitment that such housing will be made available to all those properly eligible without any discrimination based on race or creed. It must be pointed out that the federal housing agencies currently give the fullest support to state and municipal legislation guaranteeing equal opportunity in housing. But federal agencies must not support existing local legislation or custom that requires discrimination.

In short, if those responsible for the administration of federal housing forthrightly declare their intention to comply with the national policy of non-discrimination and then formulate practices and regulations that are consistent with that declaration of policy, they will do much to insure equality of housing opportunity for all throughout the country.

Every piece of federal legislation dealing with a federal housing program should include, ideally, a provision re-asserting that in this program the constitutional requirement of equal treatment under the law will be observed. The inclusion of such a provision is not essential if the Constitution is observed as living law. However, the affirmation of this principle may serve to drive home its importance and hopefully insure that it be honored in the observance, not in the breach.

The first state legislation dealing with housing discrimination involved public-housing projects. As far back as 1939, the state of New York included in its public-housing law a specific prohibition against racial and religious discrimination. The first legislative steps taken toward banning discrimination in private housing were by means of statutes that established publicly assisted housing programs. Such programs were called "publicly assisted" because they were built under machinery created by state law and received assistance either through partial tax exemption or through the use of the state's power of eminent domain to assemble the tract. They were made subject to specific bans on discrimination. More recently, a number of states expanded by statute the definition of publicly assisted housing to include housing built with the assistance of mortgage or other loan insurance granted by the federal government or the state.

The general coverage of these laws is housing built with state or federal aid. This includes nousing operated under the supervision of state agencies; housing that has been granted complete or partial tax exemption; housing built on land sold by the state or any of its subdivisions to the persons erecting the housing; housing built on property that has been acquired or assembled by the state or any of its subdivisions; and housing the acquisition, construction, repair or maintenance of which was aided financially by the state or any of its subdivisions. Such housing must be made available, because of the use of state power, to all persons within the state without discrimination based on race or creed.

Another state legislative approach to the problem of discrimination in housing was embodied in a statute adopted in New Jersey in 1955, which amended that state's Savings and Loan Act and its Banking Act to ban discrimination in the giving of mortgage loans. In 1957, when the Washington state legislature adopted a law barring discrimination in publicly assisted housing, it included in the statute a provision barring discrimination by financial institutions in the granting of loans on housing covered by the law. Other states have since enacted similar legislation, but true effectiveness requires many more states to follow the lead.

Still another approach attacks the problem head-on by the enactment of legislation that forbids discrimination in private housing. New York City pioneered by adopting in 1957 an ordinance barring home-owners and real estate agents from discriminating in private housing. Pittsburgh followed with a similar ordinance in 1958. These pioneer measures by two cities gave strong impetus to the movement toward the enactment of statewide fair-housing laws. Colorado took the lead in 1959; Oregon, Massachusetts, and Connecticut followed almost immediately. Two years later the number of states with laws prohibiting discrimination in private housing and providing for effective enforcement machinery had risen to nine, with Pennsylvania, New York, Minnesota, New Hampshire, and New Jersey joining.

Legislation should be enacted in every state barring discrimination in private housing. Such legislation is important. It establishes a machinery by which each state can insure to all inhabitants of the state equality of housing opportunity, a basic prerequisite to equality of opportunity in every other field of community life. It embodies a declaration of state policy against such discrimination. It brands the discriminator a malefactor. Such statutes will aid inestimably in breaking down the walls of exclusion that have imposed on our spreading cities ghetto patterns.

This is the avenue that has long been used in the employment and educational fields and, as we have seen, in each the nation is in a different stage of progress—but it is progress.

Broadly speaking, there are two kinds of anti-Semites in the United States today. The first is the conscious, blatant

hater of Jews who not only doesn't deny his feelings but actually boasts of the prejudice. More often than not, this kind
of bigot belongs to some rabble-rousing group. Frequently he
is the one who helps turn out vulgar anti-minority tracts and
sometimes writes ugly racist letters to newspaper editors or
otherwise engages in overt acts stimulated by his attitude. He
hates Jews, knows it, and is not ashamed. He is easily recognized for what he is by most other Americans.

The second type is the bigot who may be unaware that an
anti-Semitic impulse is beneath some of the actions in his
daily routine. For example, there is the resort-hotel operator
who refuses accommodations to Jews not because, "please
understand," he personally dislikes Jews but because "many
of my guests insist on the policy." As for himself, why— "some
of my best friends are Jews."

This last remark is deeply revealing. Inevitably it means
that the person who utters it really does not understand its
full implications, otherwise he would not use it. Having a
Jewish friend—or even several of them—is no evidence of an
absence of anti-Jewish prejudice; conversely, a lack of Jewish
friends is not evidence of anti-Semitism. To be an anti-
Semite, a man does not necessarily have to dislike individual
Jews, he does have to dislike all Jews in general. To be an
anti-Semite, his hostility need be directed only against the
abstract—a section of humanity numbering more than 12
million souls and known broadly as "Jews."

In short, a man may even like and admire a particular Jew
or several Jews whom he knows either personally of from
afar and still be an anti-Semite. Parenthetically, it should be
equally clear that one's dislike of a particular Jew or several
Jews does not necessarily make that person an anti-Semite,
since individual Jews have the same frailties as any other
human beings.

There is one good connotation in the unhappy phrase,

"Some of my best friends are Jews." It is that the person who utters the statement apparently realizes that anti-Semitism is not right, and that he doesn't wish to be considered anti-Jewish. Credit him for that much, but also credit the moral climate of the country in which he lives—a democracy whose mores condemn religious bigotry of any sort.

On the other side of the coin, his very use of the words may mean he is guilty of harboring some prejudice, the passive kind perhaps, of which he is not fully aware. Unfortunately, it is sometimes beneath the surface—as we have been able to see in the record set forth in this book.

Thus, to use the cliché "Some of my best friends are Jews" is to miss the point entirely. To make matters worse, it frequently serves only to embarrass the listener—especially if the listener happens to be Jewish. The significant fact is that many Jews privately use the remark, "Some of *his* best friends are Jews," to convey their belief that the person in question *is* an anti-Semite. When Jews are thought of as friends, like all other people they appreciate it, but when they are thought of as "Jewish friends," they know better.

This book has not dealt with the problem of the blatant professional hatemonger or his cohort, the amateur rabble-rouser, but primarily with the respectable American who discriminates because he has accepted without question a false Jewish stereotype created for him by someone else. The key to the correction of his prejudice is a determination as a rational human being to reject the distorted image of the Jewish people, which is an image drawn not on the basis of actual characteristics but on the ridiculous assumption that religion makes a people into a single, stereotyped, "different" kind of human.

Such a change in thinking is not easy to accomplish, emotion—and prejudice is an emotion—being most difficult to eliminate from one's thought processes. But it is not impossible to do, and it doesn't require the help of psychiatry. The essential lever is self-discipline; all one really needs is a commitment to himself to be logical.

Discrimination is morally wrong and violates the democratic ideal. But ethics aside, on a purely practical level, religious discrimination is stupidly unprofitable. It is to repeat the obvious to say that the denial of a job to an otherwise qualified Jew, simply because of his religion, is harmful to the productive capacity of the discriminatory business firm. Self-evident, too, is the fact that a resort operator who bars Jews as guests is cutting down his own gross income. And one hammers at a clearly discernible truth in arguing that a real estate operator who refuses to sell a home to a Jewish buyer is depriving himself of a sale and a potential profit. This is all self-inflicted damage on the part of the discriminator, and it can be avoided by a democratic viewpoint.

We have described at length the material disadvantages suffered by the victims, the scapegoats of religious bigotry. But we only hinted at what damage is done to the psyche of Americans who are subjected to inequality because of religious prejudice. Few people can be subjected to such psychological damage without injury to their potential as constructive human beings and, even if only in small degree, the evident contribution such persons might otherwise make as citizens. Therefore, let those who perpetrate acts of religious discrimination realize that while they are victimizing the targets of their hostilities and hurting themselves, they are also damaging the country they profess to love.

NOTES

1. John Higham, "Anti-Semitism in the Gilded Age," *Mississippi Valley Historical Review,* March 1957.
2. Arnold Forster, *A Measure of Freedom* (Garden City, N.Y.: Doubleday, 1950), p. 183.
3. Horace B. English and Ava Champney English, *A Comprehensive Dictionary of Psychological and Psychoanalytic Terms* (New York: Longmans, Green, 1958), p. 156.
4. Gordon W. Allport, *The Nature of Prejudice* (Cambridge, Mass.: Addison-Wesley, 1954), p. 14.
5. Louis Wirth, *The Ghetto* (Chicago: University of Chicago Press, 1928), p. 278.
6. A. M. Rose and Caroline Rose, *America Divided: Minority Group Relations in the United States* (New York: Knopf, 1948), p. 153.
7. William Peters, "Who Chooses the People You Know?", June 1959.
8. Vance Packard, *The Status Seekers* (New York: David McKay, 1959) , p. 268.
9. Marshall Sklare (ed.), *The Jews* (Glencoe, Ill.: Free Press, 1958), p. 309.
10. Packard (note 8), p. 280.
11. In Sklare; quoted by Ben Halpern, *America Is Different* (Glencoe, Ill.: Free Press, 1958), p. 25. (See note 9.)
12. W. L. Warner and P. S. Lunt, *The Status System of a Modern Community* (New Haven: Yale University Press, 1942), pp. 72–106.
13. Wirth (note 5), p. 95.
14. Nathan Glazer, *American Judaism* (Chicago: University of Chicago Press, 1957), p. 4.
15. Max Weber, *Ancient Judaism* (Glencoe, Ill.: Free Press, 1952), page 310.
16. Alvin Chenkin, *Jewish Population in the United States, 1957,* American Jewish Year Book, 1958, p. 13.
17. Robert P. Forman, *Jewish Welfare Federation of San Francisco, Marin County, and the Peninsula.* To be published.
18. Chenkin (note 16), p. 15.
19. G. W. Allport and B. M. Kramer, "Some Roots of Prejudice," *Journal of Psychology* (July 1946), pp. 9–39.
20. W. B. Brookhover and J. B. Holland, "An Inquiry into the Meaning of Minority Group Attitude Expressions," *American Sociological Review* (April 1952), p. 201.

21. Ruth G. Weintraub, *How Secure These Rights? Anti-Semitism in the United States in 1948;* Anti-Defamation League Survey (Garden City, N.Y.: Doubleday, 1949), p. 41.

22. Allport (note 19), p. 15.

23. Denis W. Brogan, *The American Character* (New York: Knopf, 1944), p. 103.

24. Alexis de Tocqueville, *Democracy in America* (New York: Knopf, 1944), p. 257.

25. Packard (note 8), p. 283.

26. *Ibid.*, p. 279.

27. American Jewish Committee Report, 1955.

28. Albert J. Weiss, "Resorts, A National Survey," *Barriers* (New York: Friendly House, 1958), p. 36.

29. Charles Abrams, *Forbidden Neighbors* (New York: Harper, 1955), p. 199.

30. Packard (note 8), p. 188.

31. John P. Dean, "Patterns of Socialization and Association between Jews and Non-Jews," *Jewish Social Studies* (Vol. XVII, No. 3, July, 1955).

32. Oscar Handlin and Mary F. Handlin, "The Acquisition of Political and Social Rights by Jews in the U.S.," *American Jewish Year Book* (1955), p. 74.

33. *Ibid.*, pp. 73–76.

34. I. S. MacCrone, *Race Attitudes in South Africa* (London: Oxford University Press, 1937), p. 249.

35. R. M. Williams, Jr., *The Reduction of Intergroup Tensions; A Survey of Research on Problems of Ethnic, Racial, and Religious Group Relations* (New York: Social Science Research Council, 1947; Bulletin 37), p. 4.

36. Sklare (note 9), p. 309.

37. Gandolfo *v* Hartman. 49 Fed. 181 (1892–Federal Court California).

38. Harris *v* Sunset Island Property Owners, Inc. 116 So. 2d 622 (1959).

39. Luigi M. Laurenti, *Property Values and Race* (Berkeley: University of California Press, 1960).

40. Nathan Glazer and Davis McEntire (eds.), *Studies in Housing and Minority Groups* (Berkeley: University of California Press, 1960), page 3.

41. Algo D. Henderson, *Approaching Equality of Opportunity in Higher Education* (Washington, D.C.: American Council on Education, 1955), p. 14.

42. Abstracts of Reports of the Immigration Commission (Vol. II, 1911), pp. 81–82.

43. Donald J. Bogue, *Population of the United States* (Glencoe, Ill.: Free Press, 1959), pp. 700–1.

44. *The Jewish College Student* (Washington, D.C.: B'nai B'rith Vocational Service, 1957), pp. 5–14.
45. Albert Gordon, *Jews in Suburbia* (Garden City, N.Y.: Doubleday, 1959) , p. 77.
46. *New York State Commission Staff Reports on Need for a State University* (Albany: William Press, Inc., 1948), pp. 1–56.
47. Howard A. Rusk, "Physician Shortage, II," *The New York Times* (December 15, 1959).
48. *On Getting Into College* (American Council on Education, 1949), pp. 16.
49. *The New York Times* (May 13, 1960), pp. 33, 41.
50. *On Getting Into College,* p. 16.
51. *The Jewish College Student.*
52. See, for instance, Eli Ginzberg and Ewing W. Reilley, *Effecting Change in Large Organizations* (New York: Columbia University Press, 1957).
53. Helen C. White, "Application Blanks," *Discrimination in Higher Education* (Washington, D.C.: American Council on Education, 1951), pp. 35–39.
54. President's Commission on Higher Education, *Higher Education for American Democracy* (Washington, D.C.: U.S. Gov't. Printing Office, Vol. I, p. 5, 1947).
55. Allport (note 19), p. 102.
56. Anti-Defamation League, *Toward a Democratic Campus* (Philadelphia: U.S. National Student's Association, 1955), pp. 27–30.
57. Harold Taylor, "The Ideals of American Youth," *Human Relations in Higher Education* (Washington, D.C.: American Council on Education, 1951), pp. 34–35.
58. Louis Krapin, "The Decline of Fraternity Bias," *Barriers* (New York: Friendly House, 1958), p. 78.
59. *Ibid.*
60. *Ibid.,* p. 79.
61. Webb *v* State University of New York. 348 U.S. 867 (1954).
62. 120 F. Supp. 554.
63. Alfred McClung Lee, *Fraternities Without Brotherhood* (Boston: Beacon, 1955).
64. Myron Kolatch, "The Yeshiva and the Medical School," *Commentary* (May 1960), p. 388.
65. *On Getting Into College,* p. 36.
66. Jack Star, "Our New Hospital Crisis," *Look* (March 29, 1960), p. 27.
67. Harold Braverman and Louis Krapin, "Medical School Admissions," *Rights* (February 1961).
68. Philadelphia Fellowship Commission, *Five Year Study of the Selection of Medical Students* (Philadelphia, 1957).
69. Frank Kingdon, *American Mercury* (October 1945).

70. *The Jewish College Student,* p. 50.
71. *Ibid.,* p. 51.
72. As reported by United States Office of Education Circular No. 554.
73. George Z. F. Bereday, "Intellect and Inequality in American Education," *Educational Record* (July 1958), p. 205.
74. *Encyclopaedia Brittanica* (11th ed.), Vol. XXVII, pp. 776–77.
75. Coleman R. Griffith, *Discriminations in Higher Education* (Washington, D.C.: American Council on Education, 1951).
76. Bogue (note 43), p. 705.
77. *Ibid.,* p. 707.
78. W. L. Warner and L. Srole, *Social System of American Ethnic Groups* (New Haven: Yale University Press, 1945), Chap. IV.
79. Sklare (note 9), p. 149.
80. Bogue (note 43), pp. 702–3.
81. Sam Welles, "The Jewish Elan," *Fortune* (February 1960), p. 137.
82. Sklare (note 9), pp. 73–75.
83. Nathan Glazer, *Social Character of American Jews* (Amer. Jew. Yearbook 1955), p. 24.
84. Z. V. Uriah, *Jews, Social, Educational, and Religious Development in Charleston, S.C., 1900–1950 (Reconstructionist,* March 21, 1952), p. 18.
85. Glazer, *Social Character of American Jews,* pp. 23–24.
86. Albert J. Weiss, "Case-Finding Techniques in Employment Discrimination Work." Mimeographed; files of Anti-Defamation League of B'nai B'rith, 1955.
87. Editors of *Fortune,* "Jews in America." Reprint from *Digest & Review,* February 1936.
88. "ADL Reports on Social, Employment, Educational and Housing Discrimination," *Rights* (December 1956–January 1957).
89. *Census Jewish College Students* (Washington, D.C.: B'nai B'rith Vocational Service, 1946).
90. *Recent Jewish Law Graduates Tell Their Story* (Washington, D.C.: B'nai B'rith Vocational Service, 1950).
91. Hochheiser *v* George L. Waterman d/b/a Management Personnel Agency.
92. *Employment Practices of Public Accounting Firms* (Cincinnati: Jewish Vocational Service, 1949).

INDEX

Index

●

267